MW00647194

Armed with Righteousness

Other volumes in the

BYU WOMEN'S CONFERENCE Series

By Small and Simple Things
Choose Ye This Day to Serve the Lord
In the Strength of the Lord
For Such a Time as This
Rise to the Divinity within You
A Light Shall Break Forth
The Joy of Our Salvation
The Power of His Redemption
The Rock of Our Redeemer
Ye Shall Bear Record of Me
Arise and Shine Forth
The Arms of His Love
May Christ Lift Thee Up
Every Good Thing
Clothed with Charity
Hearts Knit Together
To Rejoice as Women
Women in the Covenant of Grace
Women and Christ
Women Steadfast in Christ
Women and the Power Within
Women of Wisdom and Knowledge
As Women of Faith
A Heritage of Faith
Woman to Woman

Armed with Righteousness

Talks *from the* 2012 BYU Women's Conference

Salt Lake City, Utah

Visit us at DeseretBook.com

Library of Congress Cataloging-in-Publication Data

Women's Conference (2012 : Brigham Young University), compiler.

Armed with righteousness : talks from the 2012 BYU Women's Conference.

pages cm

Includes bibliographical references and index.

ISBN 978-1-60907-323-7 (hardbound : alk. paper) 1. Mormon women—Conduct of life—Congresses. 2. The Church of Jesus Christ of Latter-day Saints—Doctrines—Congresses. 3. Mormon Church—Doctrines—Congresses. I. Title.

BX8656.W6 2013

289.3'32082—dc23 2012043330

Printed in the United States of America

Lake Book Manufacturing, Inc., Melrose Park, Illinois

10 9 8 7 6 5 4 3 2 1

Contents

"Armed with Righteousness and with the Power of God in Great Glory"

Ruth Todd

As a young girl, maybe five or six years old, I had a pretty active imagination. More accurately, you might say I was a worrier. Often, when my parents would go out for the evening and leave us children in the care of a favorite babysitter, I worried that something would happen to them. I worried that my mother and father would never come home.

I have vivid memories of lying in my bed and hearing a siren outside and being absolutely certain that it was an ambulance coming to help my parents because they had gotten in a bad car accident and had to be rushed to the hospital. (I told you I was a worrier.)

Even though my parents returned home safely every single time, it didn't stop me from reliving this same scenario for many months. I remember the absolute terror that gripped my young heart. It was so real and so frightening to me that I dreaded my parents leaving, and I can still recall minute details and feelings about those nights in my bedroom so many years ago.

Like most of you, my good parents had taught me to pray when I was

---

Ruth Todd spent much of her career in radio and television broadcasting, including twenty-five years in local news broadcasting in Phoenix; Washington, DC; and Salt Lake City. She has taught in the communications department at Brigham Young University and is a senior manager for LDS Church Public Affairs. She is also a host for the Tabernacle Choir and for the Mormon Life program Conversations. *She serves as a stake Young Women president. She and her husband, Bryan, are the parents of five children.*

afraid. Every bit as vividly as I remember the fear that I felt, I remember what happened to me that first allowed me to experience comfort from a loving Heavenly Father who gave me an answer that I knew was directly from Him and meant specifically for me.

As I lay in my bed, consumed—almost paralyzed—with fear, I would be prompted to pray. Within seconds, I would see a scene in my mind and feel an outpouring of love and warmth that would wash over me from my head to my toes and immediately calm me and take away my dread. The scene in my mind and feeling of comfort were identical every single time this occurred. As this same experience was repeated, it became for me a personal message of peace from a loving Heavenly Father to a frightened little girl.

The years went by, and I outgrew my irrational fear. Not every single siren I heard stopped me in my tracks. Although I could no longer relive the experience no matter how hard I tried to summon it back, the memory of it was seared in my heart. I knew with every part of me that there was power in prayer and that the Comforter is real! All of my life I have known that prayer strengthens us and draws us to God, and indeed arms us "with righteousness and with the power of God in great glory."

I am humbled at the opportunity to present the theme of this conference. What a great and empowering theme for the women of the world! Notice I didn't just say the women of The Church of Jesus Christ of Latter-day Saints—you heard me right. We need the women of the *world* to be armed with righteousness and to influence those around them with the power of God in great glory. The Lord needs *all* of us. He is especially counting on you—you women who already have testimonies of the gospel of Jesus Christ. He needs us all and He needs us *now.*

This theme is part of a scripture found in the beginning chapters of the Book of Mormon, in 1 Nephi 14:14—"And they were armed with righteousness and with the power of God in great glory."

Let's get some context here. Lehi, Sariah, and their family have already left Jerusalem for the wilderness. The brothers have gone back to the city. After some failed attempts, some serious sibling rivalry, and some amazing spiritual experiences, the boys have finally secured the brass plates from Laban. The family of Ishmael has also joined Lehi's family. Both Lehi and Nephi have seen the vision of the tree of life, and Nephi, who delights in righteousness and is extremely obedient, has asked in faith to see everything. And I mean *everything.*

In his vision, Nephi is blessed to see the promised land and the coming of the Savior to his people. Nephi sees the great apostasy and he sees the Restoration of Jesus Christ's Church to the earth.

Nephi sees the building up of Zion and he sees all of us in our day. Nephi, in this unspeakable vision, sees the destiny of the kingdom of God. He even sees things he can't tell us about. In 1 Nephi 14:28, he says, "I, Nephi, am forbidden that I should write the remainder of the things which I saw and heard . . . and I have written but a small part of the things which I saw."

Nephi truly saw it all. One of the most salient parts of his vision gives us our theme for this conference. Nephi sees the Church of the Lamb of God in these latter days. He sees that there are relatively few people who are living righteously and keeping their covenants. Not only are they few in number, they're also scattered about the face of the earth. Contrast that to the vast majority of the people who, he writes, were choosing iniquity and breaking the commandments.

How do you suppose this small, scattered band of Saints could stay strong against such a tidal wave of wickedness?

Nephi tells us. "I, Nephi, beheld the power of the Lamb of God, that it descended upon the saints of the church of the Lamb, and upon the covenant people of the Lord, who were scattered upon all the face of the earth; and they were armed with righteousness and with the power of God in great glory" (1 Nephi 14:14).

That's how! God Himself arms His covenant people with all the tools we need to stand steadfastly in our places and build the kingdom of God in our time. His protection is around us as we seek to follow His will for us and stand up boldly for His purposes. We may be relatively small in number and scattered around the world, but our influence for good can be significant when it is magnified by the "power of God in great glory."

I love Minerva Teichert's painting, "Zion Ho! (Handcart Pioneers)," featuring a pioneer woman which is depicted on the program for this conference. It has become almost iconic for us as Relief Society sisters.

There she stands, one hand on her handcart and the other raised in determination toward the heavens, and perhaps toward us. Her fist pump is triumphant. We've said it before—she signals to us that "we women can do hard things!"

As I've looked at her—a lot, while preparing this talk—sometimes I think she's looking right back at me, reminding me that both she and I can be armed with God's power every day of our lives if we live up to our spiritual potential.

Our trials and our trails are different because of time and place, but our shared faith and commitment bond us immediately. We stand together as we are today, as sisters in the cause of Christ.

This summer, the young men and women in our neighborhood are planning to participate in a pioneer trek reenactment as so many of you have done in your own communities. I have been blessed to help with the planning of this event.

As I have learned and read the individual stories of these incredible men and women who sacrificed literally everything, I have been moved again and again and again. The legacy of their faith is foundational in our church today. Their sacrifices echo through the generations and give us, in our day, examples to emulate of standing boldly in the face of nearly every adversity imaginable. They share with us heroic personal narratives from which we can draw strength and hope during our most difficult days.

I daresay that most of my problems look like trail blisters in comparison to what they endured to walk west and build the Church in its early years.

I have always appreciated the pioneers on some level, and I am certainly grateful for my own pioneer heritage. But as I've become more immersed in stories that are new to me, and have read about experiences sometimes in their own words, people have really come alive to me—these mothers, fathers, sisters, brothers, children. I love them and I thank them. They too were small in number but certainly armed with the power of God. One of many women I have come to love is Elizabeth Jackson. She, her husband, Aaron, and their three young children were part of the Martin handcart company that trekked across the Great Plains in the late summer and fall of 1856.

They were at a point in their journey where food rations were scant, attacks from wolves or other wild beasts threatened their lives, and

Aaron, the husband, had become very, very ill. After barely—barely—making it across the freezing Platte River, they were met on the other bank by a storm of snow, hail, and wind.

Elizabeth had no choice but to lighten the load in that family handcart, so a good deal of her bedding and clothing had to be discarded.

Elizabeth's husband became sicker and sicker. One night he tried to eat but failed. He was too weak to even swallow. So Elizabeth put her husband to bed and lay beside him. And these are her words:

"I was extremely cold. The weather was bitter. I listened to hear if my husband breathed—he lay so still. I could not hear him. I became alarmed. I put my hand on his body, when to my horror I discovered that my worst fears were confirmed.

"My husband was dead! He was cold and stiff—rigid in the arms of death. It was a bitter freezing night and the elements had sealed up his mortal frame. I called for help to the other inmates of the tent. They could render me no aid; and there was no alternative but to remain alone by the side of the corpse till morning. . . . Of course I could not sleep. I could only watch, wait, and pray for the dawn. But oh, how those weary hours drew their tedious length along. When daylight came, some of the . . . company prepared the body for burial. And oh, such a burial and funeral service. They did not remove his clothing—he had but little. They wrapped him in a blanket and placed him in a pile with thirteen others who had died, and then they covered him up in the snow. The ground was frozen so hard they could not dig a grave. He was left there to sleep in peace until the trump of the Lord shall sound, and the dead in Christ shall awake and come forth in the morning of the first resurrection. We shall then again unite our hearts and lives, and eternity will furnish us with life forever more."

Elizabeth goes on to write about her utter devastation at being a widow with three small children, and about the horrible conditions that continued to plague this little company until help from Salt Lake arrived. She did make it to the valley, and years later she concluded her writings with these words: "The Lord has blessed me, and rewarded me with an abundance of the world's good, for all my sufferings, and has also blessed me with the highest blessings of a spiritual nature that can be conferred upon man or woman, in His holy temple. . . . I have a happy home for which I thank my Father in Heaven."[1]

After all she endured, Elizabeth ends her life with words of faith, gratitude, and testimony. Truly the examples of these incredible pioneer women of yesterday help arm us with God's power today.

Of course, our modern lives are certainly more comfortable, but make no mistake, sisters—there are pitfalls and perils around all of us every day and every night. It will take every bit as much determination and action on our parts to be latter-day fist pumpers. But we too can do hard things.

Through His prophets and the scriptures, the Lord has provided us numerous strategies, which we can employ in our own lives to ensure His protective power upon us and upon our loved ones. There are too many to list here today, but may I touch on just a few that have been powerful in my own experience.

For me, it begins with prayer. As I mentioned, I learned of its power as a young girl, but my testimony of prayer has grown stronger with each passing decade.

President Gordon B. Hinckley spoke of prayer's power to arm all of us: "How wonderful it is that you get on your knees . . . and pray in earnestness night and morning. . . . Prayer unlocks the powers of heaven in our behalf. Prayer is the great gift which our Eternal Father has given us by which we may approach Him and speak with Him in the name of the Lord Jesus Christ. Be prayerful. You cannot make it alone. You cannot reach your potential alone. You need the help of the Lord."[2]

It is also imperative that we arm ourselves each day by feasting upon the word of God. Don't let a day go by without serious study in the scriptures. I can testify that the more we read, the more we realize we need to read and the more we want to read. We can become like Nephi, whose soul delighted in the scriptures and whose heart pondered them.

We know there is doctrine and history and the gospel of Jesus Christ written in the scriptures, but today I want to testify to you, there are also answers—personal answers to *your* individual questions. The scriptures will lead us along and provide answers as we immerse ourselves in their holy words.

Service to others is also key as we seek God's power in our lives. We are counseled to serve with no thought of recognition; serve others both in and out of the Church; serve with members of our faith and serve alongside members of other faiths. With so much suffering and tragedy all around the world, it will take the efforts of all good people who share a similar vision working together to lift the downtrodden, help the needy, and succor God's children, our brothers and sisters.

We've also been counseled to acquire the skills and education that will allow us to serve in a variety of areas. From the earliest days of the Church, women have been encouraged to increase their learning and then use that knowledge to teach, influence, and serve.

President Brigham Young said, "We believe that women are useful, not only to sweep houses, wipe dishes, make beds, and raise babies, but they should stand behind the counter, study law or physics, or become good bookkeepers and be able to do the business in any counting house, and all this to enlarge their sphere of usefulness for the benefit of society at large. In following these things they but answer the design of their creation."[3]

Serve willingly, wherever and to whatever capacity you are called. Last year at Women's Conference, I had the privilege of sharing a speaking session with former Utah governor Olene Walker. Our assigned topic was "Magnifying Your Callings."

While her talk (as you can well imagine) was just excellent, all she really needed to do was stand there and tell you about her most recent church calling, at seventy-eight years of age. Her bishop had come to her house to welcome her (or so she thought) to the new ward. But no, instead, she was called to be the new ward *Primary* president—at seventy-eight. Isn't that great? To hear Sister Walker bear testimony of the joy of her calling was something I shall never forget.[4]

I can look to my own mother for a similar example. Last Easter, our family was all gathered at my parents' home in Phoenix. While I was talking with one sister in the family room, we could hear the delight in the voice of another of our sisters, who was down the hall and out of sight. "Mom!" she exclaimed. "You look adorable! That is the cutest outfit on you!" Now I was thinking my mother must have purchased a new spring outfit for Easter. But I had missed the boat entirely. Indeed my sister was right. My mom did look adorable—as she walked out in her khaki skirt, yellow button-down shirt, and, yes, den mother neckerchief.

My seventy-six-year-old mother said, "I'm off to Cub Scouts! I'll be back in a couple of hours." She proceeded to gather all of her grandsons who were in the Cub Scout age range and whisked them off with her own pack to their Easter activity. They had a ball.

What a lesson my mom taught her grown children that day. Surely no one would have faulted her had she cancelled Cub Scouts over the holiday when all seven of her children had come home from across the country to Arizona. But she didn't want to let her boys down. She loved them, and she served them with all of her heart.

No matter where we are in our life's journey, each of us has the opportunity to influence many people in our individual realms. That influence extends to people in our families, our neighborhoods, our wards, our workplaces—everywhere we go. It's our responsibility to be instruments for the Lord and empower others with the spiritual confidence and strength that we value so much.

Just a few weeks ago, I was reminded of my own responsibility as a mother when I was out shopping with my daughters. We were in the store, we were looking, and one of my daughters said, "Mom, I found something and I *really* want it." She took me around the corner and showed me what she'd found, and I could feel the spirit of our lovely morning together beginning to evaporate.

"You don't really want that," I said. (I tried the easy argument first.) "It's not very cute." (What a weak attempt.)

"Yes I do," she said. "It's so cute, and it's much more modest than most of the other items for sale." She started wearing me down. I had to dig deep.

"True," I said, "but it's still not quite within the okay zone for our family standards. What about this?" (Right here is where you try to imagine two faces looking at each other, rolling their eyes in unison, and then looking at me like I had just suggested some hideous thing out of the eighteenth century.) Then her sister jumped to her defense.

"Mom, it's pretty modest, you've got to admit."

We went back and forth, two against one, until finally I did what many worn-down mothers do in similar situations.

"Call your father," I said. "Let's see what he has to say." So we called my husband, and he said what every supportive priesthood holder says to his children: "It's up to your mother."

Touché. He was helping me step up to my responsibility. Now in his defense, he couldn't see what we were looking at, but we've had these kinds of conversations before.

"Okay," I said. "Then the answer is no." I was hoping the moment had passed. But come on—we all know our kids don't give up that easily.

"Mom," one daughter said (a new idea had just popped into her young, agile mind), "didn't you listen to conference a few days ago when a leader told us kids should make decisions and parents should let them learn from their mistakes? Huh, Mom, remember the girl who had to decide whether to play soccer on Sunday? What about that?"

This needed to end, fast.

"Well," I said, "I'll have to let you make a mistake on something else. Not this and not today." Pathetic, I know. But it was pretty much all I could come up with in the moment.

It was certainly not my best mothering moment, but thankfully on that day it was enough. We left the store without a single purchase. On the plus side, both of the girls were fine. And the experience led to a great discussion. We were able to verbalize that, more than any rule their parents could impose, what really mattered was for them to develop their own good judgment.

Why do I waffle? I only complicate things for myself and encourage my kids to try to wear me down again on another issue a different day. Children need and actually want strong parents who can set family standards and stick to them.

Strong women arm themselves, their children, and the youth over whom they have influence. Go back to your homes and in the kindest way, be stronger. Set a standard in your home and your life and stick to it. No waffling. You can do it. And you will bless others' lives in the process.

We all love the story of the two thousand stripling warriors. We all look to those mothers who had such a strong influence on their sons. There are only just a few lines that mention the mothers, but they are the critical lines that give us a clue about the character of these young warriors.

Alma 56:47–48—"They did think more upon the liberty of their fathers than they did upon their lives; yea, they had been taught by their mothers, that if they did not doubt, God would deliver them. And they rehearsed unto me the words of their mothers, saying: We do not doubt our mothers knew it."

We love those boys and we love their mothers, but have you ever stopped to wonder: *What exactly did those mothers do* so their sons knew with a surety that those women were completely faithful and steadfast in the gospel? What was it about their mothers' daily actions that led Helaman to say about the warriors, "Never had I seen so great courage, nay, not amongst all the Nephites. . . . They never had fought, yet they did not fear death" (Alma 56:45, 47).

Those few lines speak volumes to me. It is clear that those mothers' daily lives must have been living examples of faith *and* works. In addition to keeping the commandments, personal and family prayer, and studying the scriptures, I would imagine there was a great unity and shared commitment among those women. You simply couldn't have two thousand boys from one community all faithful and courageous if their mothers hadn't been unified in their love of the Savior, Jesus Christ.

It could never have worked had the women been judgmental of each other, compared themselves to each other, or spoken ill of one other. It would be just about impossible.

If we are to be those kinds of covenant women and raise those kinds of children for the next generation, we have got to be as unified as those women were. How would we stack up if we were asked to be a mother to one of the stripling warriors? I don't know about you, but I'd need to step up my game.

Another of the tools that empowers us with the glory of God is certainly the house of God—His holy temple. When we are endowed, we are blessed with God's protective power.

Our church's effort to build temples all around the world is a mighty validation of our theme scripture. If Nephi saw our day and observed how God's covenant people scattered across the earth could be armed with righteousness, surely he saw temples. The pioneers, who sacrificed nearly everything to build the Kirtland Temple, understood the importance of these buildings. In the dedicatory prayer revealed to Joseph Smith, we read the fulfillment of a portion of Nephi's vision:

"And we ask thee, Holy Father, that thy servants may go forth from this house armed with thy power, and that thy name may be upon them, and thy glory be round about them, and thine angels have charge over thee" (D&C 109:22).

In Nauvoo, pioneers sacrificed again, building a temple even when they knew they'd have to turn westward and leave it behind. They understood that the blessings of the temple endowment would give them the strength to endure the inevitable trials that lay ahead of them.

Likewise, regular temple attendance today offers us protection in the midst of our adversities. If you want to be armed with righteousness, get to the temple.

Let's recap. To arm ourselves in these latter days, we *supplicate* through prayer; we *study* the scriptures; we *serve* willingly and abundantly, using our education and acquired skills for good; we *stay strong*, and we empower those around us; and we *seek* the Lord in His holy house, the temple.

The last thing I'd like to discuss is *support*—or, in other words, no judging or grudging. As sisters in Zion, we all must work together. That's the way the Relief Society was organized in 1842, and I firmly believe that's how the Lord wants it to be. Though vastly different in many ways, we are united in the purposes of Relief Society recently reiterated in the book *Daughters in My Kingdom*. Six million strong, and in more than 170 countries, we sisters of the Relief Society work together to increase in faith and personal righteousness. Together we strengthen homes and families. Together we provide relief by seeking out and helping those in need.

Each of us is unique and walks our own individual path. Each of us is given different talents and abilities. Some of us are married; others are single. Some are divorced; others are widowed. Some of us work outside the home; some work full-time inside the home, while others do their best to balance both. Some of us sew or run marathons; others bake and blog. There are sisters who are great gardeners, readers, or writers! It takes all of us, and we don't want to be without a single one of our sisters.

Our job is not to judge another's situation or her choices. Quite the contrary. Agency and personal revelation are two of the most beautiful and ennobling doctrines in our entire church. We should celebrate the principle that each of us gets to search for the path the Lord has in mind for us.

As individuals, we can turn to our patriarchal blessings, our marvelous church leaders, and especially our Heavenly Father for inspiration, guidance, and personal revelation as we walk our individual roads.

We were not given the Holy Ghost "just in case." He is there to guide us. We are to learn the language of the Spirit and seek to understand His promptings so that we can be in tune with the Father's will for us.

In a recent conference talk, Elder Quentin L. Cook counseled us to support each other with love. Speaking about the difficult choices women have to make, he said: "These are very emotional, personal decisions, but there are two principles we should always keep in mind. First, no woman should ever feel the need to apologize or feel that her contribution is less significant because she is devoting her primary efforts to raising and nurturing children. Nothing could be more significant in our Father in Heaven's plan. Second, we should all be careful not to be judgmental or assume that sisters are less valiant if the decision is made to work outside the home. We rarely understand or fully appreciate people's circumstances. Husbands and wives should prayerfully counsel together, understanding they are accountable to God for their decisions."[5]

There is no place in Relief Society for criticism, for holding grudges, or judgment. Only compassion.

Let us apply to each other President Dieter F. Uchtdorf's recent conference admonition, and if you feel any negative feelings toward another sister or hold any grudge, "Stop it!"[6] Stop it today. You can if you choose.

There is simply no room for negativity that would drive away the Spirit from among the women of Relief Society. We sisters must be one in Christ and replace any divisiveness with a celebration of our diversity.

May I conclude with one final thought and a personal story? As a frightened child in my bed, waiting for my parents to get home from the hospital—you know, after their "car accident"—I knew from personal experience that the Lord wanted me to be happy and filled with peace. Isn't that what He told his disciples when He came to see them a final time after His Resurrection?

"Peace I leave with you, my peace I give unto you" (John 14:27). What a gift—*His* peace. It is no small thing for us to know what His peace and His joy feel like. It's not the world's peace—it's His.

Although we all will have bumps in the road so we can grow from adversity, the Lord has told us He wants us to rejoice and have joy in this life. Think about that.

As latter-day women of the Church of Jesus Christ, we are tasked with so many important responsibilities, and yet these duties are not drudgery. There is joy to be found in study, in service, in supporting and strengthening each other, and in our personal communication with our God. That is joyous. Whether we find that joy is truly up to us.

Early this year, a cousin of my mother's sent my mom a letter. It was a letter about my grandmother Elizabeth Layton Anderson. She was called Aunt Beth. It's a story our family had never heard. Here's a portion of that letter from our cousin Phyllis:

"Nearly sixty-five years ago, I drove from Tucson to the Gila Valley for the final fitting on my wedding dress. After the fitting, I visited Aunt Beth Anderson. She was so very gracious and happy to see us. I was bubbling over with excitement, and I told Aunt Beth, 'I am so happy. In a week I graduate from the University of Arizona. In five days, my fiancé arrives home from the Navy after serving the past three years in World War II. In two weeks we'll be married in the Mesa Temple, and I have a high school teaching job waiting for me.'

"Aunt Beth replied, 'I can see why you're so happy, Phyllis. But you know, you can be this happy every day of your life if you choose to be.'

"I was surprised at her answer, but gave it deep thought and determined that I would take her advice. Each morning of my life, I would wake up, thank the Lord for my blessings and then say, 'This is going to be the happiest day of my life. How can I make it so?' My children even remember me going up and down the hallway singing, 'Oh What a Beautiful Morning,' which, now they say, made them happy first thing in the morning."

She goes on, "All of my life, I've tried to make each day happy. Even now, after losing my husband five months ago and being told by my oncologist that I have an incurable cancer and have only a few months to live, I keep myself happy. I believe death will be sweet for me because I will meet my husband, our son, our son-in-law, and our grandson . . .

and of course my parents. I also look forward to seeing Aunt Beth and Uncle Guy because they always made me feel happy. For me, death will be sweet because I believe in Christ and know He will be there to judge me." Signed, Phyllis Blake Larson.[7] What a sweet reminder from my grandmother.

Two words: Choose joy. May we all live so that we may be counted among the faithful women of Jesus Christ's Church, which is the ultimate joy. And may we understand firsthand what it feels like to be "armed with righteousness and with the power of God in great glory." This is my prayer for all of the sisters of the Church.

Notes

1. Elizabeth Horrocks Jackson Kingsford, available at http://www.lds.org/library/pio_sto/Pioneer_Trail/23_North_Platte_River.html; accessed 15 October 2012.
2. Gordon B. Hinckley, "Inspirational Thoughts," *Ensign*, August 1997, 5.
3. Brigham Young, in *Journal of Discourses*, 26 vols. (Liverpool: Latter-day Saints' Book Depot, 1854–86), 13:61.
4. See Olene S. Walker, "Called to the Primary—At Seventy-Eight," in *By Small and Simple Things: Talks from the 2011 BYU Women's Conference* (Salt Lake City: Deseret Book, 2012), 166–71.
5. Quentin L. Cook, "LDS Women Are Incredible!" *Ensign*, May 2011, 21.
6. Dieter F. Uchtdorf, "The Merciful Obtain Mercy," *Ensign*, May 2012, 75.
7. Personal correspondence in author's possession.

Discipleship and Our Ministry

Sandra Rogers

Those of us who are members of The Church of Jesus Christ of Latter-day Saints find it difficult to understand why so many today say that we are not Christians. They attempt to explain away our faith and our commitment to the Savior by telling us that we don't really worship or follow Jesus because our revealed understanding of the nature of God the Father, His Son, Jesus Christ, and the Holy Ghost differs from theirs.

The most obvious and compelling answers to these criticisms are probably not found in a detailed discourse about our doctrine, although the faithful and articulate women of the Church could provide such responses. The answers, instead, are found in the Savior's instructions to those who followed Him during His lifetime.

Prior to the agony of Gethsemane and the brutality of the cross, those closest to Jesus were met together for the Passover supper. After that meal, Jesus washed their feet, including the feet of Judas Iscariot, and taught them, "A new commandment I give unto you, that ye love one another; as I have loved you, that ye also love one another. By this shall all men know that ye are my disciples, if ye have love one to another" (John 13:34–35). Then He explained, "If ye love me, keep my commandments"

Sandra Rogers is the international vice president at Brigham Young University. She has taught Sunday School and served a mission to the Philippines; She is a member of the Relief Society general board and chair of the BYU Women's Conference committee.

(John 14:15). Jesus also taught that "by their fruits ye shall know them" (Matthew 7:20).

Succinctly our Savior outlined the sum of Christian worship; it is to love Him, to love each other, and to keep His commandments. From these fundamentals flow all the other Christlike virtues. This is why, when President Gordon B. Hinckley was asked, "What is the symbol of your religion?" he replied, "The lives of our people must become the most meaningful expression of our faith and, in fact, therefore, the symbol of our worship."[1]

After recounting the Savior's life, teachings, suffering, and ultimate Resurrection, President Hinckley concluded, "And so, because our Savior lives, we do not use the symbol of His death as the symbol of our faith. But what shall we use? No sign, no work of art, no representation of form is adequate to express the glory and the wonder of the Living Christ. . . . As His followers, we cannot do a mean or shoddy or ungracious thing without tarnishing His image. Nor can we do a good and gracious and generous act without burnishing more brightly the symbol of Him whose name we have taken upon ourselves. And so our lives must become a meaningful expression, the symbol of our declaration of our testimony of the Living Christ, the Eternal Son of the Living God. It is that simple, my brethren and sisters, and that profound and we'd better never forget it."[2]

In 1982, an important addition was made to the title of the Book of Mormon—"Another Testament of Jesus Christ." If our lives are to be a meaningful symbol of our devotion to the Savior, then we must come to the determination, in soul, heart, and mind, that we too will be another testament of Jesus Christ; that by our fruits—our thoughts, our words, our deeds—others may know Him whom we love, whom we strive to follow, and whom we try to obey.

Early in His ministry, many were impressed by Jesus' miracles, including the feeding of the five thousand, and they followed after Him, hoping for continual bread and fish. Jesus tried to explain that He was offering them the way to eternal life, not a daily meal. Consequently, "from that time many of his disciples went back, and walked no more with him" (John 6:66) because it was "an hard saying" (John 6:60). When Jesus saw those who had deserted Him, He asked the Twelve, "Will ye also go away?" Peter's answer was, "Lord, to whom shall we go? thou hast the words of eternal life" (John 6:67–68).

Like Peter, our decision to be a disciple is founded on the simple truth that Jesus Christ has the words of eternal life. Where else would we go? One of the definitions of *disciple* is "any follower of Jesus Christ," and the word *follow* means to accept another as a leader, a guide, an acceptable authority, someone to use as an exemplar. Jesus is our exemplar, and we started on the road to discipleship when we were baptized and took upon us His name, recognizing that "there shall be no other name given nor any other way nor means whereby salvation can come unto the children of men, only in and through the name of Christ, the Lord Omnipotent" (Mosiah 3:17).

We elevate our discipleship to another level when we make sacred covenants in the temple. By making and keeping these covenants, we bind ourselves "to act in all holiness" (D&C 43:9) and gain access to His power and blessing in our lives. In direct revelation to Sister Emma Smith, the Lord said, "All those who receive my gospel are sons and daughters in my kingdom" (D&C 25:1). Receiving His gospel is accepting that wonderful absolute truth that Christ came to do the will of the Father, that He suffered immense agony in the Garden of Gethsemane and on the cross of Calvary and then arose from the tomb and conquered death and hell, that because of this epitome of charity we can become changed creatures, alive in Him, and return to His presence and enjoy a life like His, with the sociality of our loved ones, friends, and fellow servants in His work. In return for our willingness to bind ourselves to Him, He has promised us that in His strength we can do all things, that through Him we can find peace, and that in His promises we can find hope and comfort.

These are the truths that offer us sanctuary in times of persecution, assurance when we have moments of doubt, conviction when our courage may be tested, resolve when we face difficulties, and mercy when we feel alone, discouraged, or that somehow we have not "measured up."

Ours is not a religion that is merely contemplative. If it were, thinking about tithing would be just as beneficial as paying it. Analyzing chastity and virtue would be the same as being chaste and virtuous. Studying all the many aspects of charity would be the same as being charitable.

And dissecting all the pros and cons of service would be the same as actually doing deeds of service.

Consequently, our discipleship is most often manifested not in our thoughts but in the things we do and the traits we develop. In fact, our discipleship is made manifest in our ministering. One definition of *ministering* is acting as the agent or the instrument of another. Our discipleship is demonstrated in the ways we are the Lord's instruments and when we act as His agents. Sometimes we accept callings and assignments to be the Lord's instruments. We teach classes, we prepare activities for youth, we preside in organizations, and we visit teach. Sometimes we are the Lord's agents in the roles we have as mother, aunt, grandmother, sister, niece, or cousin. And many times over we are the Lord's agents because we are trying to be like Jesus, and we're trying to be in tune with His voice and reflect His Spirit in our lives at home, at work, and in our neighborhoods.

Women are not always featured in the scriptures. But I believe the words Jesus spoke to women in the scriptures affirm how well He knows and loves His disciple daughters and how much He wants them to understand the gospel plan and follow Him.

Three of the women Jesus knew best and loved the deepest were His mother, Mary, and His dear friends Mary and Martha. The New Testament records the experience the family of Joseph and Mary had when they discovered Jesus was not with them on a return trip from Jerusalem. His absence caused His mother grave concern, and she reacted as any mother would. When she found Him, she let Him know they were worried! He'd caused His parents some problems. His gentle answer was, "Wist ye not that I must be about my Father's business?" (Luke 2:49). In other words, did His mother remember His important mission and allegiance?

Later, during His ministry, He visited the home of His good and dear friends Lazarus, Mary, and Martha. All of us can relate to Martha's growing exasperation with her sister. My guess is that it had happened before. Martha's talents lent themselves to serving, and Martha was slugging it out in the kitchen alone, perspiring over a hot fire, clanging pots and pans, juggling the preparation of the food, wanting it to be just perfect for a favored guest, getting more and more frustrated, and building up a good head of steam about her sister, who was not helping. Jesus understood Martha and her feelings. He acknowledged those feelings when He told her that He knew she was worried about many things. And then He gently reminded her that choosing Him, choosing the "good part" (Luke 10:42), was the most important.

In these exchanges with the women He knew best and for whom He had the most tender feelings, we can see that the Savior understands women. He knows they worry. He knows they "sweat the small stuff." He knows they want their labor in caring and worrying and being cumbered about to be acknowledged and appreciated. And He also knows that they will be happier if they learn to choose the "good part."

I recall a devotional I attended at Brigham Young University when I was a student (one of the few I recall from my time there). Sister Elaine Cannon described a time when her husband was a bishop. It was fast Sunday. The ward meetings were over, and she was home preparing dinner. Her husband was supposed to come home at a certain time for dinner but did not. She described how, as the roast got drier and drier and the vegetables got soggier and tougher, her frustration with her husband grew.

She was near volcano proportions when the thought entered her mind: *My husband has been fasting too. He is a big man. He's probably really hungry. If he could have, he would have been home by now.* These thoughts calmed her troubled and frustrated heart. When her husband finally did come through the door, he immediately apologized and then told her about a sweet and wonderful spiritual experience he had just had with a ward member. She told us how grateful she was that she had reined in her frustration before he arrived, because had she not, she would have spoiled the tender, spiritual sharing moment she had with her husband.[3]

I also believe that Jesus understood that women can magnify their imperfections far better than they often magnify even their callings. Women can dwell on their mistakes and churn in the tide of guilt and inadequacy over many things, believing they will never be good enough or that they can never be restored to the good person they really wanted to be.

But Jesus offers women hope when they struggle with these feelings. He has the power to help us turn our weaknesses into strengths. He offers a helping hand, a way up, not a condemnation that keeps us down, perseverating on our shortcomings. You see, He doesn't want to lose any of us. Why do you think He tells the parables of the creditor and the debtors, or the lost sheep, or the prodigal son? He's trying to tell us that He wants all of us to pass mortality with flying colors.

Remember Martha, who judged and complained about her sister Mary? She learned to choose the good part. She relied on the encouragement Jesus gave her. When Lazarus died, she met Jesus with a changed heart. He was not just a family friend. She knew that He was "the Christ, the Son of God." And sometime later when Jesus visited their home, we're told that while Mary anointed Jesus' feet with ointment, "Martha served," no longer troubled by her hurt feelings (John 12:2).

Jesus wanted women to know that their faith would be rewarded. Remember the woman who had suffered from a hemorrhage for twelve years? She didn't expect special attention or even a formal blessing. She simply said "within herself, If I may but touch his garment, I shall be whole" (or free from disease). Jesus felt her touch, the touch of a faithful woman, and responded to her, saying, "Be of good comfort; thy faith hath made thee whole" (Matthew 9:21–22).

Jesus understood that women like to know that their efforts are good and acceptable. He especially wants them to know they can be acceptable to Him. He knew that women want to be seen as making good decisions. That's why some examples of Jesus' interactions with women found in the scriptures are there to confirm that the careful choosing of Him and His doctrine will always be acceptable, no matter what someone else does or says.

We see this in His rebuke to His disciples who chastised a woman who had poured precious ointment on Him. They thought it was a waste, that the ointment should have been sold to help the poor. He instead said, "Why trouble ye the woman? For she hath wrought a good work upon me. . . . Verily I say unto you, Wheresoever this gospel shall be preached in the whole world, there shall also this, that this woman hath done, be told for a memorial of her" (Matthew 26:10, 13).

In other words, when the world tells us that we're nuts for raising children in the gospel, trying to have scripture study, family prayer, and family home evening; for trying to fit in a temple session when we could have been shopping or working out to maintain our body beautiful or attending a "pay attention to me" night instead; for learning every trick in the book to keep hems at the knees—and necklines in the right places—instead of being fashionable and chic; for taking the time to visit teach that sister who is so hard to catch rather than watching the latest popular show on television; for giving up grandchildren and the Winnebago to make a difference as a senior missionary couple; for working hard to follow the new handbook even when many sisters are demanding to just keep doing things the way they've always done them—all we need to do is remember that the Lord said, "for them that honour me I will honour" (1 Samuel 2:30).

Because the original Twelve Apostles were called disciples, we may imagine that we have to occupy an important position or have a highly visible ministry in the Church to really be disciples. Nothing could be further from the truth. While those who are General Authorities and officers of the Church and serve in leadership positions in wards and stakes are often the most noticeable or prominent examples of the heart and soul of discipleship, it is really in the regular, salt-of-the-earth members who go about their daily lives with faith, hope, and charity that we see discipleship in action. These members have the faith to know that the Savior did what He said He would do. They have the faith that through the plan of salvation and the Atonement, all that God has will eventually be theirs. They have the faith that through repentance they can be acceptable to God and receive all of His blessings in eternity. That faith, a confidence in the King of Kings, is a wellspring of courage and security and motivation. With it comes hope, a perspective on the present and the future that is bright and open, and seeking for the light, no matter what the circumstances are. As hope endures, faith increases. And as faith and hope grow and develop, we begin to experience a "change of heart." We feel "to sing the song of redeeming love" (Alma 5:26). And when this happens we receive His image in our countenances.

Discipleship is about emulating Jesus. There are many stories of Jesus healing the sick and afflicted. One I especially like is "when Jesus was come into Peter's house, he saw his wife's mother laid, and sick of a fever. And he touched her hand, and the fever left her: and she arose" (Matthew 8:14–15).

Jesus saw a need and responded. He didn't wait for Peter's

mother-in-law to send a request for a blessing to the bishop. He didn't wait for someone to call the Relief Society president, who would then assign visiting teachers to bring in a meal and report back. He didn't check the Church handbook to see if it was His place to help or whether the problem should be turned over to someone else. He didn't assume that someone else would surely show up, sooner or later, and provide aid. He simply met the need He saw.

Disciples invest in others when they meet needs. How many stories have we heard about members who help sponsor a missionary; of priesthood holders who make sure the sons of single mothers are included in outings and other priesthood functions; of those individuals who just see a need, like my dear neighbor Jared, who shoveled the snow from my driveway far more often than being a good neighbor required.

I have experienced many such investments by willing disciples. One was Sister Gwennie Webb. I was called to play the organ for Sunday School when I was in junior high. Sunday School in those olden days was a ninety-minute meeting with talks and singing time along with the lessons. Sister Webb was a chorister who believed in teaching us how to follow the chorister. She loved to change tempos. She loved to change volume. I was a very inexperienced organist. I could play the piano, but I had never tried to play the organ. There were three basic things a Sunday School organist needed to have: hands to play the keyboard, feet to play the pedals, and eyes to follow the chorister.

That first Sunday I was having such a hard time with the hands and feet part that I was abysmal on the "eyes to follow" part. I was not a success by any stretch.

After my wretched performance, Sister Webb asked if I would like to learn to follow. She said she could teach me to follow the chorister, and she could also teach me to be an accompanist. Little did I realize there is a difference between being a pianist and being an accompanist. She invited me to come to her home one day each week after school where she taught me and tutored me in following the chorister and in accompanying groups or soloists. I don't think that was part of her Sunday School assignment—but she definitely saw a need and was willing to make a sacrifice to make an investment in a young, thirteen-year-old sister.

I have learned that true disciples do anything to find a way to be obedient. They never look for excuses or a way out of an obligation. They just find a way to be obedient. One of my dearest fellow missionaries was Sister Perla Manuel. She was a schoolteacher at the time of her conversion, supporting her aging parents, who had many health problems.

She wanted to obey the law of tithing, but all of her salary went for the care of her parents. Her strategy was to crochet. She would come home from school, attend to her parents, fix dinner, do what was needed around the home, and then stay up late into the night crocheting. She would then sell the doilies and table runners she'd made, and with the money earned, she paid an honest tithing. She found a way. Think of how this applies to so many things in our lives—visiting teaching, temple worship, scripture study, family prayer, magnifying callings, missionary efforts. Did I say visiting teaching? Disciples always find a way.

True disciples also embody charity, the "pure love of Christ" (Moroni 7:47), which motivates them to love others and extend charity and goodness to them. Charity has two sides. One side is our love for our Savior and Redeemer, and this love is the foundation of our discipleship. And the other side is His love for us, manifest in His atoning sacrifice and His patience and compassion and care.

Elder Marvin J. Ashton observed: "Perhaps the greatest charity comes when we are kind to each other, when we don't judge or categorize someone else, when we simply give each other the benefit of the doubt or remain quiet. Charity is accepting someone's differences, weaknesses, and shortcomings; having patience with someone who has let us down; or resisting the impulse to become offended when someone doesn't handle something the way we might have hoped. Charity is refusing to take advantage of another's weakness and being willing to forgive someone who has hurt us. Charity is expecting the best of each other."[4]

Disciples are kind and considerate. They are patient and long-suffering. They bear with hope their afflictions. But they also reach out to help others bear up as well. I think of the story of President Spencer W. Kimball helping that frazzled mother in an airport who had a tired and crying child. Just as the priest and the Levite walked by the wounded man on the road to Jericho, the other passengers waiting to board the plane were either too embarrassed to connect themselves with the miserable mother and child or just too protective of their own time and comfort. President Kimball instead was anxious to provide care and compassion.[5]

Another hallmark of a true disciple is the capacity to have mercy, a capacity that includes kindness and pity, and benevolence, and generosity and tolerance, but especially forbearance and forgiveness. We're under injunction in the Doctrine and Covenants to forgive all—because all of us are in need of forgiveness, especially from God (see D&C 64:10). And yet forgiveness may be difficult for us to offer.

The parable of the unmerciful servant is one that often pricks my own conscience. Peter asked the Lord how often he was supposed to forgive, suggesting that seven times would be his limit. Jesus responded that "seventy times seven" was a more accurate number. Then He gave the parable of the unmerciful servant. A servant owed his master ten thousand talents and could not repay the debt. Consequently the master ordered that he and his family be sold into slavery and all that he had confiscated for the payment. The servant begged for patience and mercy, and it was granted. Now here comes the sad part.

"But the same servant went out, and found one of his fellowservants, which owed him an hundred pence: and he laid hands on him, and took him by the throat, saying, Pay me that thou owest. And his fellowservant fell down at his feet, and besought him, saying, Have patience with me, and I will pay thee all. And he would not: but went and cast him into prison, till he should pay the debt." When the master learned of this, he called the unmerciful servant "wicked," and asked, "Shouldest not thou also have had compassion on thy fellowservant, even as I had pity on thee?" Then the master "delivered him to the tormentors, till he should pay all that was due unto him" (Matthew 18:28–34).

Jesus made sure that no one could misunderstand the parable, saying, "So likewise shall my heavenly Father do also unto you, if ye from your hearts forgive not every one his brother their trespasses" (Matthew 18:35).

Years ago I was in a very difficult situation where I felt criticized and undermined, and I felt I could do nothing to change the situation. I began to harbor harsh feelings. I could feel resentment, anger, and frustration building up inside of me, and I knew it wasn't good.

Later, in preparing for an assigned talk (isn't this the way it always works?), I was led to the scriptures in the Doctrine and Covenants and in

Matthew that I have just quoted. I began to count the many times I had gone to my Heavenly Father begging for his forbearance and forgiveness for my sins and shortcomings. I recalled the times when I had needed to go to others to ask for their forgiveness. I admit that my first thoughts in this situation were not merciful; they were selfish. I said to myself, *Well, this is certainly a bummer of a deal. If I can't forgive these people who are making my life miserable, I give them power to keep me from being forgiven, and I don't want those jerks to have that kind of power over me.* Not exactly charitable or merciful, but somehow it was the beginning of breaking the chains I had been wrapping around myself so I could eventually let go and be free. That's when I learned that forgiveness is a gift you give yourself as much as a gift you give another.

Sometimes the things we are asked to forgive are large and significant and may include abuse, infidelity, dishonesty that creates economic hardship and loss, injustice, withdrawal of a loved one, or the suffering of a loved one. But more often, we're asked to forgive smaller, pettier offenses that simply hurt our pride. But I testify that, in either case, the Lord will help us do it.

Disciples also never think they "have it made." They endure to the end in humility and hope. They are never armed with self-righteousness. Let me give an example to illustrate this point. When I was a Laurel, my class decided that we wanted to go to general conference. We had car washes and bake sales to try to earn the money to travel from Arizona to Salt Lake City. Seven of us, our Laurel teacher, Analee Westover Hunsaker, her husband, Theo, and their baby crammed ourselves and our luggage into a station wagon for the trip, leaving after school on Friday. We encountered a huge snowstorm on the way and arrived in Salt Lake around 2:00 A.M. We checked into a small motel on south State Street, with plans to wake up at 5:00 A.M. in order to get seats in the Tabernacle. But we were so exhausted we slept through the alarm, and we didn't arrive on Temple Square until about seven-thirty.

We had just missed the first wave of seating in the Tabernacle. We stood in line in our Arizonan Easter dresses and sandals, hoping to be among the few that finally made it into the building. It was snowing; it was wet; it was cold—it was April conference—and we were freezing. But there was a good-natured camaraderie in our line.

After about thirty minutes, a good brother who had a seat inside came to the doorway and gazed down at us. He smiled broadly as he told us that he already had a warm seat inside. He shared with us the one thing that none of us had ever thought of—if only we had come earlier, we too would be inside where it was warm. Then he went back in, only to return regularly to repeat his message. I remember one person in our line muttering something about the Zoramites and a Rameumptom. The ushers tried to keep our spirits up, and one did suggest to the man that he might be safer if he just stayed in his seat. Ultimately, we did get in at the last minute and sat behind the choir. The thrill of being in the presence of prophets, seers, and revelators was sweet warmth for our frozen toes and healing balm for our resentment of the man with the early seat.

But since that Saturday just over forty-four years ago, I have often reflected on this experience and used it as a yardstick of my own behavior. Has there ever been a time in my desire for righteousness that I lost sight of the Living Christ as the one I should be emulating? Was there ever a time that I stood in the warmth of the doorway and "looked down" in judgment on someone who was standing in cold, wet snow?

At the beginning of His ministry, Christ attended the synagogue in his hometown of Nazareth. As was the custom, He was invited to read the scripture passage for that day, which came from Isaiah. He read, "The Spirit of the Lord is upon me, because he hath anointed me to preach the gospel to the poor; he hath sent me to heal the brokenhearted, to preach deliverance to the captives, and recovering of sight to the blind, to set at liberty them that are bruised." He then announced, "This day is this scripture fulfilled in your ears" (Luke 4:18, 21).

This is our charge—to preach the gospel, His gospel, in the way we live each day; to demonstrate in our lives our love for the Lord and our devotion to His Holy Name and to His cause, which is the cause of righteousness. We are here to do His work, to be His instruments. Like Him, we are here to heal, to deliver, to recover, and to set free. Our lives are the most powerful sermons that we can ever preach—especially in our families and our homes, but also to our neighbors and our communities. In fact, they may be the only sermons some will ever hear. We're never off duty when it comes to being disciples of the Lord Jesus Christ.

We are poor in pride because we are humbled by the grandeur of the gospel and the magnificence of the Atonement and our own constant need to beg at the mercy seat. We are humbled that our Father offered His Only Begotten Son to heal us and bring us home, and so we want to reach out to others who feel lost, wounded, forgotten, troubled, or misplaced.

We rejoice even when there are times to mourn because we know He offers peace and comfort, and we want to extend that same compassion to others.

We are meek because we recognize the source of our strength and know that we "can do all things through Christ which strengtheneth" us (Philippians 4:13), especially when it involves caring for those within our circle of watchcare and ministering.

We hunger and thirst after righteousness because we know if we will open our minds and hearts, the Holy Spirit will teach us—teach us of Christ—and will help refine and justify and purify and sanctify us as we are covered by His power.

We are merciful because we know He is merciful toward us and how much we are in need of His mercy.

We are pure in heart because we know that personal cleanliness in heart and mind, in motivation and in deed, is the key to having the Lord's Spirit with us always and being able to enter into His presence.

We are peacemakers because we know that Christ's light and influence does not come where there is contention and that by following His light we can ultimately be like Him and always be with Him.

We are willing to be persecuted for righteousness' sake because we believe His promises to us are sure, and that the kingdom of God offers far more than any other, worldly enticement.

Not long ago, because of another assignment, I was asked to read a book titled *Half the Sky*.[6] It is a positive book about attempts to help women in the world, but it is also a chronicle about the oppression of women around the globe. It tells stories of women who are treated like chattel, who are bought and sold into slavery, who are seen as the spoils of war. It is a chronicle of how Satan views women—as nearly worthless. When I had finished the book, I walked out of my office and laid it on the desk of my assistant, and I noticed the contrast with the two books that were now side by side on her desk.

We have been given a marvelous new resource that tells us how God feels about women, and how much the Lord loves His daughters. This book, a contrast to how Satan would like the world to feel about women, shows us the principles, precepts, and patterns that lead us to a life of discipleship in following the Savior, Jesus Christ, because God our Father loves us and our Savior loves us deeply. *Daughters in My Kingdom*[7] is a testimony that the Lord's servants have vision, because it has come forth in a time of confusion and misrepresentation about who we are, and what we are worth as women, and what should be important to us, and about what the Lord needs us to do to be part of His work.

It testifies of His love for us. It teaches of our grand capacity. It is a template for virtue and service. It tenaciously affirms that He will bless us with strength, wisdom, revelation, spiritual gifts, and charity as we serve Him through our service to others in and out of the Church. And it tenderly reassures us that He knows us well, that He needs us to provide earthly watchcare in charity to each other.

It is a triumphant message that the covenant women of the Church, "armed with righteousness and the power of God in great glory" (1 Nephi 14:14) can prevail—can prevail over any and all mortal challenges. It has come "for such a time as this" (Esther 4:14) so that we will understand the incredible role women have in the Lord's holy work as they increase in faith and personal righteousness, strengthen home and family, seek out others, and provide relief.

As they were leaving Nauvoo and their beloved temple behind, a group of our Latter-day Saint forebears wrote this message on a wall in the temple: "The Lord has beheld our sacrifice: Come after us."[8] Now let us do the same for the next generation. Through our sacrifices as His disciples, let us "bring forth the blessings of heaven" for our day and our time. Let us be the kind of people Jesus will want to claim as His. Let us love Him more. Let us feed His sheep. Let us care for His lambs.

Then we will be disciples who are "more fit for the kingdom,"[9] and our fruits will testify that we are His, true Christians in heart, soul and mind. May He bless us in this effort to follow Him.

Notes

1. Gordon B. Hinckley, "The Symbol of Our Faith," *Ensign*, April 2005, 3.
2. Ibid., 6.
3. Elaine Cannon, "Male, Female, and the Lord," Brigham Young University devotional, 10 February 1970, audio recording; available at http://www.podfeed.net/episode/Male+Female+and+the+Lord+Elaine+Cannon/310661; accessed 15 October 2012.
4. Marvin J. Ashton, "The Tongue Can Be a Sharp Sword," *Ensign*, May 1992, 19.
5. See Edward L. Kimball and Andrew E. Kimball Jr., *Spencer W. Kimball: The Early and Apostolic Years* (Salt Lake City: Deseret Book, 2006), 334. See also the obituary of "the woman in the airport," Sharon Elaine Morgan, who passed away in August of 2012, available at http://www.deseretnews.com/article/765594797/Obituary-MORGAN-SHARON-ELAINE.html?pg=all; accessed 15 October 2012.
6. See Nicholas D. Kristof and Sheryl WuDunn, *Half the Sky: Turning Oppression into Opportunity for Women Worldwide* (New York: Vintage Books, 2010).
7. See *Daughters in My Kingdom: The History and Work of Relief Society* (Salt Lake City: The Church of Jesus Christ of Latter-day Saints, 2011).
8. In Heidi S. Swinton, *Sacred Stone: The Temple at Nauvoo* (American Fork, Utah: Covenant Communications, 2002), 136.
9. Philip Paul Bliss, "More Holiness Give Me," *Hymns of The Church of Jesus Christ of Latter-day Saints* (Salt Lake City: The Church of Jesus Christ of Latter-day Saints, 1985), no. 131.

Remember Who You Truly Are

Mary N. Cook

What a blessing to meet together, to learn together, and to feel the Spirit testify of things that matter most. In today's world *to know who you truly are* is probably one of the most important principles we can learn for ourselves and then teach our children. It may matter the most. Understanding our identity will greatly influence our choices, our happiness, and ultimately our destiny. Confusion about our identity is one of Satan's greatest tools, and he has a multitude of methods to mix us up. The topic of identity is one that has concerned me greatly, especially in working with young women. It is probably at the top of the list of helping a young woman become truly converted, live the principles of the gospel, be worthy to make and keep sacred covenants, and prepare for her most important roles as wife and mother.

For your awareness, I would first like to explore some of Satan's tantalizing tactics that he is using to wage his all-out war on women. I would then like to spend some time discussing how we as women—armed with righteousness and with the power of God—can counter Satan's attack on

---

Mary N. Cook is the first counselor in the Young Women general presidency. Prior to her call, she served as second counselor in the presidency and as a member of the Young Women general board. Sister Cook received bachelor's and master's degrees and an EdS degree from Brigham Young University. She was a special education teacher and administrator and an elementary school principal. She became a stepmother to four children and step-grandmother to seventeen grandchildren when she married Elder Richard E. Cook, a former member of the Seventy, in 1988.

us, which is aimed not only to frustrate our individual eternal progression but also to dismantle eternal families.

Analogy of the Mixed-Up Chameleon

Let me begin by telling you about a children's story by Eric Carle entitled *The Mixed-Up Chameleon.* As I tell you about this story, identify the gifts and strengths of the chameleon. How does he perceive his gifts and strengths? What are the traps that he has fallen into? Are we, as women, falling into these same traps?

Like any chameleon, this chameleon was able to change its appearance at will according to its environment. In the story, the chameleon found himself at a zoo, where he began to envy and covet the other animals and change his appearance to match that of the other animals. After a while, the chameleon became a little mixed-up and adopted pieces of each of the other zoo animals. Moreover, he was hungry, but because of all the changes that had occurred, he was unable to do that which he was born to do. Let's read the story from here:

> *Just then a fly flew by.*
> *The chameleon was very hungry.*
> *But the chameleon was very mixed-up.*
> *It was a little of this and it was a little of that.*
> *And it couldn't catch the fly. . . .*
> *I wish I could be myself.*
> *The chameleon's wish came true. And it caught the fly!*[1]

Did you see yourselves in this story? What had the chameleon forgotten? His identity! He had forgotten the very thing that made him unique and was most important for his survival. His ability to change colors protected his life from predators. His long, sticky tongue kept him alive. He focused on the things he wasn't and had forgotten all that he was.

The Sexualization of Women

It is easy for each of us to become this mixed-up chameleon in our world of movies, television, fashion magazines, and advertisements, which bombard us with messages of who we aren't or who we should be. The media teach us that what matters most is how we look, never revealing to us that the unrealistic images we see are enhanced by airbrushing and computerized tweaking. The pitch is, "If you buy this cream, try these diet pills, buy this dress, you can look like this, and . . . you'll be a happy chameleon!" These persistent messages cause us to doubt our worth and camouflage our real purposes here on earth.

Elder Jeffrey R. Holland addressed his concerns about these confusing messages. In a recent conference address entitled "To Young Women," he said: "In too many cases too much is being done to the human body to meet just such a fictional (to say nothing of superficial) standard. As one Hollywood actress is reported to have said recently: 'We've become obsessed with beauty and the fountain of youth. . . . I'm really saddened by the way women mutilate [themselves] in search of that. I see women [including young women] . . . pulling this up and tucking that back. It's like a slippery slope. [You can't get off of it.] . . . It's really insane . . . what society is doing to women.'"[2]

This is the sexualization of women. "Sexualization occurs when someone's sense of their own value is based solely on sex appeal or that individual is held to narrow standards of attractiveness." Sadly, the "sexualization [of women] has been going on for decades, largely unnoticed, the elevator music of American life."[3] We must start noticing the music not only because of the detrimental effects it is having on our identity but because of the negative repercussions on our rising generation.

A series of articles published last fall in the *Deseret News* by Lois Collins and Sara Lenz addressed the topic of sexualization and how this media blitz is negatively affecting the identity of our little girls and young women. The hours and hours our children are being exposed to these kinds of media are taking their toll. They said that even "little ones, ages 2 to 11, average 32 hours [of TV each] week. Those 12 to 17 average 23 hours. . . . During those hours, they'll drink in ads for hair products and teen-siren TV shows, makeup and technology, much of it couched as 'hot' or 'sexy. . . . '

"Children and teens are becoming 'sexualized' and researchers and psychologists say it hits girls particularly hard, shaping their view of themselves and their potential, as well as how others view them." The experts say that "it affects [their] 'identity, behavior and opportunity.'"[4] This is a very heavy price to pay.

It may seem an insurmountable task to stop this profusion of propaganda, but we can turn away from it and focus our attention and the eyes of our youth to those who are doing good rather than looking good. Audrey Barshich, author of the book *All Made Up,* said: "As a society, we know more about women who look good than we know about women who do good. . . . The most celebrated women today are famous primarily for being thin and pretty, while women who are actually changing the world remain comparatively invisible."[5]

As women of virtue, we must become visible. We must drown out the elevator music, trumpeting that which is virtuous, lovely, and of good report. As we are promised in Doctrine and Covenants 121:45, virtue will give us confidence and qualify us for the Holy Ghost to guide us in speaking out against this pervasive evil. President Joseph F. Smith gave us a charge when he said that "he expected the sisters 'to lead the world and . . . especially the women of the world, in everything that is praiseworthy, everything that is God-like, everything that is uplifting and that is purifying to the children of men.[6]

OUR IDENTITY

Preparation for this counterattack will require us to individually be certain of—and never forget—our own divine identity. To change the world, specifically the homes and communities in which we live, we must remember who we truly are and help those we love know who *they* truly are. Let us focus today on all that we truly are.

First and foremost, "we are daughters of our Heavenly Father, who loves us."[7] I have always loved the Wordsworth poem quoted by President Thomas S. Monson in the April 2012 general conference:

Our birth is but a sleep and a forgetting:
The Soul that rises with us, our life's Star,
Hath had elsewhere its setting,
And cometh from afar:
Not in entire forgetfulness,
And not in utter nakedness,

But trailing clouds of glory do we come
From God, who is our home:
Heaven lies about us in our infancy![8]

We come to earth trailing clouds of glory. We come with several gifts from God that we must always remember. The plan of salvation is a gift. The privilege to come to earth and receive a body—a sacred temple—is a gift. The opportunity to learn through our moral agency, through test and trial, is a gift. The enabling power of the Atonement of our Savior, which helps us to become all that He knows we can become, is a gift. The redeeming power of the Atonement, which rescues us from our frailties and mistakes, is a gift. Our gender, determined long before we came to earth, with its attending possibilities, potential, and unique purposes to create life and nurture, is a gift. The fact that our Father in Heaven knows our names, our circumstances, our "hopes and dreams, including [our] fears and frustrations"[9] is a gift. Elder Jeffrey R. Holland reminded us of our greatest gift when he said: "Because of this divine heritage you, along with all of your spiritual sisters and brothers, have full equality in His sight and are empowered through obedience to become a rightful heir in His eternal kingdom, an '[heir] of God, and joint-[heir] with Christ'"[10]—an incomprehensible gift!

Spiritual Gifts

These are gifts and opportunities universally given to each of us. In addition, each of us came to earth with at least one unique spiritual gift. Spiritual gifts are "special spiritual blessings given by the Lord to worthy individuals for their own benefit and for them to use in blessing others."[11] Our spiritual gifts are the attributes that we must remember and never forget. In Doctrine and Covenants 46 we learn about spiritual gifts. Beginning with verse seven, we receive specific instructions that teach us how to deal with Satan's campaign to deceive us and of his desire to have us stray from our divine destiny: "But ye are commanded in all things to ask of God, who giveth liberally; and that which the Spirit testifies unto you even so I would that ye should do in all holiness of heart, walking uprightly before me, considering the end of your salvation, doing all things with prayer and thanksgiving, that ye may not be seduced by evil spirits, or doctrines of devils, or the commandments of men; for some are of men, and others of devils" (D&C 46:7).

Isn't this what the media is doing—seducing us (interesting word, isn't it?) with the doctrines of the devil? We then learn that our spiritual gifts are what will help us to not be deceived and to benefit us and others: "Wherefore, beware lest ye are deceived; and that ye may not be deceived seek ye earnestly the best gifts, always remembering for what they are given; For verily I say unto you, they are given for the benefit of those who love me and keep all my commandments, and him that seeketh so to do; that all may be benefited that seek or that ask of me, that ask and not for a sign that they may consume it upon their lusts" (D&C 46:8–9).

Now, verse ten—the message I hope you take with you—to always *remember* your gifts: "And again, verily I say unto you, I would that ye should always remember, and always retain in your minds what those gifts are, that are given unto the church [or to you]" (D&C 46:10).

We then learn specifically about these gifts, that we don't have all the gifts, but that each gift is unique and has a specific purpose. As I slowly go through this list, I would like you to identify your spiritual gifts, or the spiritual gifts of your spouse, your children, or the sisters for whom you are responsible:

> For all have not every gift given unto them; for there are many gifts, and to every man is given a gift by the Spirit of God. To some is given one, and to some is given another, that all may be profited thereby. To some it is given by the Holy Ghost to know that Jesus Christ is the Son of God, and that he was crucified for the sins of the world. To others it is given to believe on their words, that they also might have eternal life if they continue faithful. And again, to some it is given by the Holy Ghost to know the differences of administration, as it will be pleasing unto the same Lord, according as the Lord will, suiting his mercies according to the conditions of the children of men. And again, it is given by the Holy Ghost to some to know the diversities of operations, whether they be of God, that the manifestations of the Spirit may be given to every man to profit withal. And again, verily I say unto you, to some is given, by the Spirit

> of God, the word of wisdom. To another is given the word of knowledge, that all may be taught to be wise and to have knowledge. And again, to some it is given to have faith to be healed; and to others it is given to have faith to heal. And again, to some is given the working of miracles; and to others it is given to prophesy; and to others the discerning of spirits. And again, it is given to some to speak with tongues; and to another is given the interpretation of tongues. And all these gifts come from God, for the benefit of the children of God. (D&C 46:11–26.)

Did you identify your gift or your loved ones' gifts? Now, I didn't specifically see the gift that was identified in my patriarchal blessing on that list, but there are many spiritual attributes identified in Doctrine and Covenants 4. They include "faith, virtue, knowledge, temperance, patience, brotherly kindness, godliness, charity, humility, [and] diligence" (D&C 4:6).

Elder Russell M. Nelson taught us in his April 2012 general conference address: "The attributes by which we shall be judged one day are all spiritual. These include love, virtue, integrity, compassion, and service to others. Your spirit, coupled with and housed in your body, is able to develop and manifest these attributes in ways that are vital to your eternal progression."[12] We can develop these attributes.

I have to remind myself often of my gift and work on my other spiritual attributes. I must remember that the purpose of that gift is "for the benefit of the children of God" (D&C 46:26). Our spiritual gifts should be our focus. These are the attributes we must identify in ourselves and in our children and develop to bless those around us.

Now, following the pattern of President Dieter F. Uchtdorf, I would like you to please apply the following: If you, like our chameleon, are doubting your abilities as a woman, a wife, and a mother, doubting your testimony, doubting your ability to lead, or wondering about your gift—*stop it!*[13] You must not only remember your gifts but also remember that the enabling power of the Atonement of Jesus Christ makes it possible to do all things. Remember the promise, "In the strength of the Lord thou canst do *all* things" (Alma 20:4; emphasis added). Look to Him for help. Pray to continually remember who you are.

If you are being tempted to focus your time and energy on your body and your looks—*stop it*! Focus on keeping your body well and healthy. Love your body for its capabilities and all it has done and can do to bless the lives of others, including being a cocreator with God, one of the greatest gifts given specifically to women.

If you define the worth of others by their outward appearance—*stop it!* Focus on the divine attributes of others. When you see a young woman, resist the temptation to compliment her on how cute she looks. Let her know of the ways her life is blessing others, her kindness toward the less popular, or her courage in living the standards. Help her remember her spiritual gifts.

If you find yourself filled with envy for a gift you don't have—*stop it!* Elder Jeffrey R. Holland said it best when he told us, "We are not in a race against each other to see who is the wealthiest or the most talented or the most beautiful or even the most blessed. The race we are *really* in is the race against sin, and surely envy is one of the most universal of those.

"Furthermore, envy is a mistake that just keeps on giving. Obviously we suffer a little when some *misfortune* befalls *us*, but envy requires us to suffer all *good fortune* that befalls *everyone* we know! . . . Coveting, pouting, or tearing others down does *not* elevate *your* standing, nor does demeaning someone else improve your self-image. So be kind, and be grateful that God is kind. It is a happy way to live."[14]

In closing, I would like you to take a moment and write down your spiritual gifts or attributes. What do you do well? What characteristics are yours that bless the lives of others? Don't be modest. Others who know and love you may easily identify them. Ask your mother, your sister, or your friend what they perceive as your gifts. Perhaps, like our mixed-up chameleon, you have forgotten them. Continue to work on your list and pray about the spiritual attributes you have or would like to develop. Keep it near you and refer to it often. Always *remember* who you truly are.

I still struggle with my identity—don't we all? It is the tug-of-war between the natural man and God. When I was a nine-year-old girl, my mother enrolled me in elocution lessons because she was concerned with my identity. She wanted her shy daughter to do things far beyond what I thought I could do, and she thought these lessons would help give me confidence.

In one of my classes we were asked to memorize poetry. I did this not knowing that when I turned sixty and started to see the weight shift, the lines deepen, and the aches ensue, I would start to understand the meaning of this poem by Karle Wilson Baker:

> *Let me grow lovely, growing old—so many fine things do:*
> *Laces, and ivory, and gold, and silks need not be new;*
> *And there is healing in old trees, old streets a glamour hold;*
> *Why may not I, as well as these, grow lovely, growing old?*[15]

I bear witness that we are daughters of our Heavenly Father. He sees us as lovely, and we should too. Armed with righteousness and the power of God, may we keep that divine identity in sharp focus so that we will be able to choose that which matters most. May we resist the pressures of the world and recognize Satan's tactics to erode our divine identity and purposes. May we as righteous women initiate the counterattack by remembering the gifts that God has given to us and to those we love, that we may remain strong and be not deceived. Indeed, may we always *remember* who we truly are.

NOTES

1. Eric Carle, *The Mixed-Up Chameleon* (New York: Harper Trophy, 1988).
2. Jeffrey R. Holland, "To Young Women," *Ensign*, November 2005, 30.
3. Lois M. Collins and Sara Lenz, "The End of Innocence: The Cost of Sexualizing Kids," *Deseret News*, 18 September 2011; available at http://www.deseretnews.com/article/print/700180194/The-end-of-innocence-The-cost-of-sexualizing-kids.html; accessed 15 October 2012.
4. See ibid.
5. Audrey Barshich, cited in ibid.
6. Joseph Fielding Smith, in *Daughters in My Kingdom* (Salt Lake City: The Church of Jesus Christ of Latter-day Saints, 2011), 66.
7. Young Women Theme, in *Young Women Personal Progress* (Salt Lake City: The Church of Jesus Christ of Latter-day Saints, 2009), 3.
8. William Wordsworth, "Ode: Intimations of Immortality," from *Recollections of Early Childhood* (Boston: D. Lothrop and Company, 1884), 23–24.
9. See Holland, "To Young Women," 28.
10. Ibid.

11. Guide to the Scriptures, "The Gifts of the Spirit"; available at http://www.lds.org/scriptures/gs/gifts-of-the-spirit?lang=eng&letter=g; accessed 15 October 2012.
12. Russell M. Nelson, "Thanks Be to God," *Ensign*, May 2012, 79.
13. See Dieter F. Uchtdorf, "The Merciful Shall Obtain Mercy," *Ensign*, May 2012, 75.
14. Holland, "The Laborers in the Vineyard," *Ensign*, May 2012, 32.
15. Karle Wilson Baker, "Let Me Grow Lovely," *Texas Woman of Letters: Karle Wilson Baker* (College Station, TX: Texas A&M University Press, 2005), 175.

"Be Not Afraid, but Speak"

Jane Clayson Johnson

Several years ago I chuckled at the results of a survey of American attitudes toward certain professions. "How would you feel," the question was worded, "if a doctor, lawyer, banker, policeman, accountant, mechanic, etc., moved in next door?"

The survey revealed that respondents placed television news reporters way down at the bottom of the list—in a dead heat with attorneys! I hope that my days in TV news are far enough behind me that I'll be welcomed as your neighbor as we spend some time together.

Although I refer to this survey with humor, the question it poses really is worth thinking about. What if we turn the tables and make *you* the new neighbor? Is it possible that your neighbors could hold a grudge simply because you're a teacher, a doctor, a stay-at-home mom, or even a news reporter? Maybe your neighbors don't really care much about your profession, but they do care about your religious beliefs.

Which makes me wonder what the results of *this* survey might be: "How would you feel if a Mormon moved in next door?" Some possible responses:

1. "Delighted! Mormons really know how to treat their neighbors."

Jane Clayson Johnson is a former national TV and radio host at CBS News, ABC News, and NPR. She is the author of I Am a Mother. *She and her husband, Mark W. Johnson, are the parents of five children and live in Boston.*

2. "Indifferent. And it's funny you should ask. I found out last week that my neighbors of fifteen years are Mormons. I had no idea!"

3. "Fired up! I plan to march right over there so I can enlighten them. Do you realize how stifling their religion is?"

4. "Mortified! Mormons are among the least charitable people I know."

Today I wish to tackle these fictional—but not unrealistic—responses.

How do we stand tall and speak up for who we are as Latter-day Saints? How can we be firm and immovable in the wake of peer pressure and yet avoid self-righteousness?

Before we get started, let's quickly take a look at what people know about us. Pollster Gary Lawrence conducted a nationwide survey of American adults and learned that 98 percent have heard of our faith. But their knowledge about us as a people and as a church ranged from mostly accurate to appalling, mostly because more than half of Americans reported that they do not personally know an active member of the Church.[1]

Simply being a Mormon sets each of us up for a certain amount of judgment. I'm certain most BYU Women's Conference attendees are not labeled by their neighbors as the "least charitable person" they know. But do your neighbors know you're a member of The Church of Jesus Christ of Latter-day Saints? Do you live your life in such a way that they can see that you are at least a little different from the world at large?

What do you do if they express their pity—quite mistakenly, of course—that you belong to "a church that sees women as second class" and "restricts so many of your freedoms," both comments a former neighbor once made to me.

It can be difficult to stand up and proclaim the truth, especially if you're in the minority, viewed as "old-fashioned," even "closed-minded." Sometimes, it's easier to live "in camouflage,"[2] as Elder Quentin L. Cook put it, not letting people know who we are or what we believe.

This is, of course, just exactly what Satan would have us do.

Elder Jeffrey R. Holland put it quite bluntly when he said, "Satan cannot directly take a life. That is one of the many things he cannot do. But apparently his effort to stop the work will be reasonably well served if he can just bind the tongue of the faithful. . . . I ask for a stronger and more devoted voice, a voice not only against evil . . . but a voice for good, a voice for the gospel, a voice for God."[3]

Why is it so hard? And how do we do it?

To borrow the words from a well-known Primary song, we "follow the prophet."[4] We do what President Thomas S. Monson called a "simple yet far-reaching formula": "Fill your minds with truth. Fill your hearts with love. Fill your lives with service."[5]

Fill Your Minds with Truth

The best place I know to find the truth is in the scriptures, which are full of stories about people just like you and me who quickly—and perhaps with a bit of feigned humility—say, "Oh, I can't do that. No, not me." When what they're really thinking is, "I'm scared to death to stand up and speak!"

Consider the Old Testament story of Gideon. The Lord called Gideon to deliver the children of Israel from bondage after seven years of captivity. "Go in . . . thy might," He says. "Thou shalt save Israel . . . Have [I not] sent thee?" Clearly, the Lord sees something special in Gideon. But what is Gideon's response? "My family is poor in Manasseh, and I am the least [of] my father's house" (Judges 6:14–15).

Sound familiar? "Me? A voice for God? Really? I'm just an average, churchgoing, doing-the-best-I-can-but-nobody-of-real-importance person." Right? Well, Gideon thought he too was weak and incapable. But God saw Gideon as valiant and inspiring—a man who had filled his heart with truth, and with a little prodding, he expounded that truth and liberated the Lord's people from bondage.

My husband and I recently met a radiant young woman who had filled her mind with truth that empowered her with confidence. She was a soon-to-be graduate of Brigham Young University–Idaho on a stage waiting to speak about her plans for the future. She was petite, with curly blonde hair, and before she spoke, I thought to myself, *Boy, that girl is "lit from within"!* When her turn came, she talked about discovering her potential. Then, with a huge smile, she quietly but very clearly said: "I want you to know I'm learning many things here. But most importantly, I've learned to be a disciple of Christ." That woman was so clearly unashamed of her faith, of her devotion to seek out the truth, that you could feel it.

Each of us can gain that same confidence by filling our minds with truth. Because in order to proclaim the truth, we must first have it emblazoned on our minds and in our hearts. And then, as Paul was taught, "Be not afraid, but speak" (Acts 18:9).

Be not afraid, but speak.

Elder M. Russell Ballard cautioned that "many misunderstandings and false information about the Church are somewhat our own fault for not clearly explaining who we are and what we believe."[6] If each of us in this room were able to overcome our fears and clearly and knowledgeably explain "who we are and what we believe," can you imagine the impact?

Many have been willing to give their lives to stand for truth. Another example from the Old Testament: Remember the infamous king Nebuchadnezzar. He erected a glorious and massive golden idol and placed it in the middle of town with instructions for everyone in the land to gather and bow before his idol. "The princes, the governors, and captains, the judges, the treasurers, the counsellors, the sheriffs, and all the rulers of the provinces" were present, the scriptures say. And they were commanded, when "ye hear the sound of the cornet, flute . . . and all kinds of musick . . . fall down and worship the golden image that . . . the king hath set up. And whoso falleth not down and worshippeth shall . . . be cast into the midst of a burning fiery furnace" (Daniel 3:3–6).

So, the music starts, and on cue, the crowd indeed falls to its knees. Everyone falls . . . *except* three men: Shadrach, Meshach, and Abednego. They alone stand tall. In a fit of rage, the king has these three men thrown into the fiery furnace. Clearly, a terrifying outcome!

Fortunately, these days, there is little to no chance that we'll be asked to stand in front of a massive, golden idol and bow down or be cast into the flames. But there are other idols, unseen or merely symbolic, to which the music plays and everyone around you starts to change their posture.

These idols appear in the form of political correctness, peer pressure, the promise of worldly success, astounding new technologies, and the list goes on and on—as could our fears, if we believe that standing tall means we'll be stranded in a sea of bowing enemies waiting to throw us into the flames. But we cannot and must not be afraid to stand alone. We have made a covenant, as did the people of Alma, to "stand as witnesses of God at all times and in all things, and in all places" (Mosiah 18:8). That means even when it gets a tad uncomfortable.

I recently had an opportunity to make a public choice: Do I sit silently, "in camouflage," as others define an issue or a conversation? Or do I stand up for my beliefs, defend my values, and articulate a position that's not only in the minority but unappreciated and even "politically incorrect"?

It happened in a meeting with some smart, influential decision-makers. At one point the conversation turned to fostering diversity at this particular institution. What started as a discussion about being more inclusive quickly spiraled into a somewhat frenzied attempt to insure that different pet groups and projects received more than an equal share of attention. The comments seemed to completely throw out diversity of faith and culture in favor of more popular, modern expressions of diversity. And frankly, I wasn't prepared for some of the comments that followed. I sat in my seat, thinking very carefully about what I was going to do, how I might articulate my position forcefully and clearly, yet thoughtfully and with respect. Finally, I raised my hand to respond. I was measured, somewhat clumsy at times, to be sure—I could feel myself shaking inside. But I managed to insert a few remarks about our family's faith, about the importance of including people of all faiths—if we were really seeking true diversity. I went home feeling a little shaken but glad I hadn't sat there in silence. And to be perfectly honest with you, I wondered if I would I be labeled or even ostracized from this group.

Then the e-mails came. One read: "Your comment in the meeting on the many shades of diversity was more than welcome to my ears." Another woman wrote that this particular issue was "often twisted to a large degree. Thanks for bringing it to the forefront and so tactfully. Can I sit by you next time?"

Even though I felt like the lone voice in that meeting, it turns out I was not alone.

Those who said nothing but felt just like I did were validated, given a voice. And I have a sense that they'll feel empowered next time to speak up themselves.

FILL YOUR HEARTS WITH LOVE

I learned another important lesson that day. *What* we say is important. *How* we say it is critical. We will have greater success and increased acceptance and understanding of our message if our hearts are full of love and respect for others.

President Gordon B. Hinckley said, "The true gospel of Jesus Christ [has] never led to bigotry. It [has] never led to self-righteousness. It [has] never led to arrogance. The true gospel of Jesus Christ leads to brotherhood, to friendship, to appreciation of others, to respect and kindness and love."[7]

The Savior Himself said, "Love one another; as I have loved you" (John 13:34). There are no exceptions, no conditions, no waivers in that commandment. If we want to make a difference, we must truly love our neighbors, open up to them, let them see into our world. As you do this, I promise that you will be surprised at how many common allies you find. We're not alone in trying to change the world for good.

I recently sat on a panel at Tufts University in Boston. There were three of us on the stage: a Jewish woman, a Muslim woman, and me, a Mormon woman. We had been asked to talk about our faith and how it defines us as women. There were many interesting discussion points centered on our religious doctrines and how the world sometimes views them—and us—as unusual, even peculiar. As the conversation deepened, I found it fascinating that the three of us had so much in common—not doctrinally, but by the mere fact that the strength of our beliefs had led each of us to goodness. Imagine what could be accomplished in the world if we were to pull together in friendship and truly work with like-minded people who are *not* of our faith but who stand for right!

Elder M. Russell Ballard reminds us of the Savior's teachings: "We are all neighbors and . . . we should love, esteem, respect, and serve one another despite our deepest differences—including religious, political, and cultural differences. . . . Of all people on this earth," he said, "we should be the most loving, the kindest, and the most tolerant because of [our] doctrine."[8]

Think about how our lives would improve if our main concern was not who is right but how can I be a friend? How can we find common ground? How do we form friendships outside of our cultural and religious circles?

I'll never forget the advice of an astute visiting teacher. I was bemoaning the endless task of cleaning a house left in chaos by little children. "Start in a corner," she said.

Start in a corner.

Take a little corner of your world and try it. Try first reaching out to those on your street or in your office or at the park. As you develop new and real friendships, barriers will fall. You won't feel the need to put on any camouflage. You will share your faith as freely as any other part of your heart.

In 1999, Elder Marlin K. Jensen said, "Consider the power of each . . . of us, 10 million strong, of our own free will and choice reaching out to those not . . . of our faith in unconditional friendship."[9]

Yes, imagine the power! Unconditional friendship. Speaking truth without sounding self-righteous. Being tactful and considerate of others' feelings. As Paul taught the Corinthians, it's better to speak five words that teach than ten thousand in an unknown tongue that may dazzle but not edify (see 1 Corinthians 14:19).

Fill Your Life with Service

Sometimes—many times, in fact—we need not say anything at all, because our *actions* will speak most loudly.

A wonderful and very effective bishop in one of the wards in my stake famously challenged his congregation to "live the gospel in your community, not just in your home and in your private life."

Our ward mission leader envisions every member of the congregation incorporating a nonmember in their church calling. He tells of a sacrament meeting "bread coordinator" who asked her nonmember neighbor to teach her how to bake bread for her congregation every week. That sister then branched out and found other neighbors who taught her to make different kinds of bread for Sunday worship. They all had a new appreciation of that holy ordinance after many accepted invitations to church.

I also love the story of women in Irvine, California, who are helping their children to be proud of who they are and what they believe—by serving—quite literally, serving lunch! It's famously called "Mormon Lunch." About every week, these moms whip up a buffet for up to sixty teenagers, a feast of taco soup, chicken nuggets, lasagna—whatever it is, lots of it! About a third of the teenagers who come are LDS. Two-thirds are not. The only rule? The first five kids through the door have to organize a blessing on the food. It's consistently the nonmember kids who arrive first and sometimes stumble through a prayer, but who happily oblige. Dessert consists of the famous "Sweet Treats" in a basket by the door—a little yummy something with a scripture attached and a thought about a gospel principle that the kids are studying in seminary.

Speaking of seminary, attendance at "Invite a Friend Day" in Irvine has increased fourfold because of Mormon Lunch. Many of the nonmember kids now want to go to Church dances. "I didn't know Mormons were allowed to dance!" one of the girls proclaimed to her friends at lunch. She and some of the other girls even went online to find out LDS dress standards to make sure that they were appropriately prepared.

Kym Henderson helps carry on the tradition of Mormon Lunch with some other moms. She told me, "We can see how it emboldens our kids. They're now less intimidated to speak up about what they believe. Those kids are in our homes. They feel of our goodness. Bottom line, our kids don't have to hide who they are."

CONCLUSION: THE POWER OF TRUTH, LOVE, AND SERVICE

None of us has to hide who we are! Will it take some work to throw off the camouflage and move out into the open? Absolutely! But we can do it. Truth. Love. Service. There is no other combination that reaps such rewards. And what are the rewards? I propose that among them is a little change in the results of that hypothetical survey I referred to earlier: "How would you feel if a Mormon moved in next door?"

"Well, I'd be thrilled. The Mormons I know are strong and immovable in their faith. But they are also loving, kind, respectful, and ever-willing to make a positive difference in their community."

Let's throw off our camouflage. Let's live our lives in a way that we can courageously speak out for truth and righteousness with humility and respect—communicating the good news of the gospel of Jesus Christ. He lives. He loves us. This I know for sure and I will be forever proud to declare it.

NOTES

1. See Gary Lawrence, *Mormons Believe . . . What?! Fact and Fiction about a Rising Religion* (Orange, CA: The Parameter Foundation, 2011).
2. Quentin L. Cook, "Live by Faith and Not by Fear," *Ensign*, November 2007, 72.
3. Jeffrey R. Holland, "We Are All Enlisted," *Ensign*, November 2011, 44–47.
4. Duane E. Hiatt, "Follow the Prophet," *Children's Songbook* (Salt Lake City: The Church of Jesus Christ of Latter-day Saints, 1989), 110–11.
5. Thomas S. Monson, "Choose You This Day," *Ensign*, November 2004, 70.
6. M. Russell Ballard, "Faith, Family, Facts, and Fruits," *Ensign*, November 2007, 25.
7. Gordon B. Hinckley, "The BYU Experience," BYU devotional address, 4 November 1997; available at http://speeches.byu.edu/?act=viewitem&id=761; accessed 15 October 2012.
8. M. Russell Ballard, "Doctrine of Inclusion," *Ensign*, November 2001, 37.
9. Marlin K. Jensen, "Friendship: A Gospel Principle," *Ensign*, May 1999, 65.

Be Proud of Who You Are and What You Believe

Carri P. Jenkins

Shortly before the end of 2011, I heard Amanda Dickson on KSL Radio pose this question: "If you had to pick one word to sum up 2011 for you, what would it be?" Amanda explained that she was prompted to ask this question, in part, by the story of Merriam-Webster's chosen Word of the Year. All morning I thought about Amanda's question, but I also asked myself, "What do I want *my* word to be for the coming year?" In all honesty, my first choice was *sleep*. But my next choice was the word *listen*.

I vowed that instead of being the first to pipe up when I felt something was inaccurate or misinterpreted, I would wait for further information. Rather than greeting my children or my husband on the phone with a barrage of questions or a litany of my plans, I would inquire first about what they were up to. And, particularly when it came to matters concerning the Church, I decided that I would put myself in the shoes of those who are trying to better understand and learn who we are before passing judgment.

Part of the reason for my goal probably came from a recent experience

---

Carri P. Jenkins is the assistant to the president for University Communications at Brigham Young University. In that position, she serves as the spokesperson for the university and directs the university's communications offices. Carri received bachelor's and master's degrees from BYU. For twelve years, she served as the associate editor of BYU Magazine, *the university's alumni publication. She serves as the Laurel adviser in her ward's Young Women organization. She and her husband, Paul, are the parents of two children.*

with my good friend and fellow running partner. For several years, three of us have been running together before the crack of dawn. Usually we have all of the world's problems solved by 6:00 A.M.; it's just amazing to me that more politicians—or I should say *any* politicians—have not called us. Anyway, one morning we were discussing a burning news item, which focused on accusations that The Church of Jesus Christ of Latter-day Saints is a cult. "How could anyone think this way?" I asked. Tracy, who is not a member of the LDS Church, responded, "Do you really want to know?" For the next several miles, Tracy explained that when we utter certain words and phrases, this is what she hears. She assured Kim and me that she did not believe the Church is a cult, but she also helped us see how our own words can be misunderstood.

I will always be grateful for the opportunity I had to listen to Tracy that morning. And I wanted more opportunities like this one, where I took the chance to really listen. So with that resolve, it was interesting to receive a few days later a letter from the BYU Women's Conference committee with an invitation to speak about "being proud of who you are and what you believe." As I read the description of the assigned topic, stopping on such words as *firm* and *immovable*, I wondered how I could possibly juxtapose my new goal of listening with this bold declaration I had been asked to speak upon.

I was particularly drawn, however, to the questions: "How can we be firm and immovable in the wake of peer pressure and yet avoid self-righteousness?" "What are ways that we can be a 'voice for the gospel'?"

President Gordon B. Hinckley counseled us: "There is a great need for civility and mutual respect among those of differing beliefs and philosophies. We must not be partisans of any doctrine of ethnic superiority. We live in a world of diversity. We can and must be respectful toward those with whose teachings we may not agree."[1]

Micheal Flaherty, who founded Walden Media and has produced such blockbuster family-friendly films as *Charlotte's Web*, *Holes*, and the Chronicles of Narnia series told the *Deseret News* that he "doesn't view faith as a mechanism for separating people along denominational lines, but rather sees it as an inclusive force that can unify via common beliefs." In other words, he said, "We need a motley crew to change the world."[2]

Each one of us—whether we live in American Fork, Utah, as I do, or in Massachusetts, as my fellow presenter Jane Clayson Johnson does—has the opportunity to be a part of what Flaherty called a "motley crew." We live in a world of diversity and differing beliefs. We live in a world where neighbors, coworkers, and family members come together for the greater good of our communities every single day—despite our differences.

A few months into preparing for today, Jane and I both discovered that we were going through the same internal struggle. Recognizing the counsel President Hinckley has given to us, we wrestled with our prescribed title. Finally, I realized that I was adding words to this title and description. Nowhere did it say, "Aggressively and obnoxiously be proud of who you are!" Likewise, it didn't say, "Be so firm and unbending that you never consider others' opinions or thoughts or needs—just drown out their voices with your own!" Through prayer and study, I also came to the conclusion that perhaps wrestling the need to be courageous and bold with the need to be humble and understanding is a necessary part of our own development in becoming a voice for the gospel.

For my own sake in attempting to organize my thoughts, I have categorized this process of giving voice to our beliefs into what I have termed "the four Ss": seep through, salute the Savior's teachings and example, speak up, and slide on.

Since January, my niece Emilie has been studying at the Brigham Young University Jerusalem Center. Her parents have been kind enough to copy me on her e-mails home. In February, Emilie shared with us a personal challenge she has given herself. Quoting a motto of one her professors, Emilie wrote, "What do you know and how do you know it? The meaning behind that is that sometimes in the Church we focus so much on the *application* of doctrine that we lose the doctrine. Tradition and other cultural aspects take over true principles. This question, 'What do you know and how do you know it?' teaches us to look for the real motivations behind why we do things so that we can have a strong foundation."

Emilie goes on to say, "It's made me want to 'be . . . an example of the believers, in word, in conversation, in charity, in spirit, in faith, in purity' (1 Timothy 4:12), like so many of these good people are, whether they are LDS or not. I hope to leave here being fully immersed in what I know and how I know it, so that it seeps through me entirely and I do things because it is the Lord's will and not because it's 'what everyone else does' back home."[3] I have had the good fortune of living close to Emilie her entire life, and I can tell you that everything she has learned in Primary, Sunday School, Young Women, seminary, and at Brigham Young University seeps through her.

As President Hinckley admonished, our lives "must become the most meaningful expression of our faith" and "the symbol of our worship."[4] It seems to me that if the goodness of the gospel does not seep through us, yet we boastfully put on the armor of righteousness, we are nothing more than hypocrites. But when we put on that armor and the metal of that breastplate reflects what is in our hearts, we have created a protective casing that cannot be penetrated by false accusations and lies, no matter how unfair or hurtful they may be. The beauty of this armor is that it prevents us from overreacting to every little jab that comes our way. We are able to stand with confidence and love and patience and share "what we know and how we know it." Does this mean that we need to be perfect before sharing the gospel? Absolutely not.

Emilie's dad could probably tell you that my dear niece has a few flaws. Yet a sincere desire to have our outer countenance reflect the righteous desires—and I would emphasize *desires* here—of our heart is exactly what Paul counseled when he said, "Be . . . an example of the believers" (1 Timothy 4:12).

The believers, as we know, are the followers of Christ—those who've willingly, with much sacrifice, put aside old views, thoughts, and customs, and opened their minds and hearts to a new and greater appreciation of what it means to love our neighbors. This wasn't easy for Christ's disciples, even those closest to Him, and it's certainly not something that is without challenge for us today. Having a father in the army, I learned early on what it meant to salute a higher-ranking officer. A salute meant you acknowledged that officer, you respected that officer, and you would follow him or her into battle.

When we sing the Primary song, "Love One Another,"[5] do we fully accept and agree to follow the divine principle the Savior teaches in John 13? Elder Quentin L. Cook has explained that in emphasizing love and unity, the Savior was not simply "teaching a [lesson] in ethical behavior." Speaking of the Savior's charge to His disciples at the Last Supper to love one another, Elder Cook says, "This was the Son of God pleading with His Apostles and all disciples who would come after them to remember and follow this most central of His teachings."[6]

"As we listen to the messages of this conference," Elder Cook said at the April 2010 general conference, "we will be touched in our hearts and make resolutions and commitments to do better. But on Monday morning we will return to work, school, neighborhoods, and to a world that in many cases is in turmoil. Many in this world are afraid and angry with one another. While we understand these feelings, we need to be civil in our discourse and respectful in our interactions. This is especially true when we disagree. . . . If we show love and respect even in adverse circumstances, we become more like Christ."[7]

It is also important to remember that when we seek to live as Christ did and as He taught, we will be blessed with the gift of discernment. If anyone had this gift, it was Esther of the Old Testament.

Just recently some very dear friends gave me a beautiful picture of Esther. I thought I knew Esther. For me, she represents all that a spokesperson should be as one who willingly "stands up and speaks out." Yet Esther, upon hearing of Haman's request to authorize a royal decree to annihilate the Jews, did not go storming off into the king's quarters—nor did she shrug her shoulders and say, "But what can I do? After all, the king's already banished one wife."

Esther literally followed Elder M. Russell Ballard's advice to engage without being defensive.[8]

In her case, engaging meant talking over what we assume was a delicious meal—a tactic that has worked for more than one woman. I always thought that when Esther asked the Jews to fast and pray with her that it was simply for strength and courage; I now believe that Esther was also praying for discernment, to determine when the right moment would occur to tell the king of Haman's plan. Perhaps this is why she held her tongue until the second feast.

At times, however, we don't always have the luxury of a second feast. As Elder Ballard has counseled us, "If we want to be respected today for who we are, then we need to act confidently—secure in the knowledge of who we are and what we stand for, and not as if we have to apologize for our beliefs"[9]—something Esther certainly exemplified.

In my job at Brigham Young University, I have found that there are instances when we have a very small window to correct a misperception or an outright falsehood. Like you, I have had the opportunity to talk with people who rather rudely criticize and condemn our faith. In these instances, I always pray for discernment.

I will never forget picking up the phone many years ago at the end of a very long week to immediately have a reporter with a large, national paper launch into a diatribe against our BYU students. Let me assure you that most reporters do not represent themselves this way and work hard to be objective and fair. But perhaps he had had a long week as well. (The angel on my shoulder tells me to say that.)

He went on and on about the fact that he didn't believe BYU was a real university and that our students were simply sheep. It was at that point, I had had enough.

I can tell you that before this call I had never raised my voice with a reporter. And I wasn't screaming, but you could have clearly heard me from across or down the hall. I remember telling this reporter, "Don't you dare call our students sheep. These students come to BYU from all fifty states and from 120 countries. They are often the only members of the LDS Church in their high schools. They know what it's like to go to a party and get up and leave—completely alone—because alcohol or illegal drugs are being passed around. Does this sound like a group of sheep to you?"

He didn't answer my question. What he said was, "Are you on the record with all of this?"

"You bet I am," I said.

I then hung up the phone and walked out into the hall outside my office. I remember looking up and down, thinking, "Boy, it's been nice working here." Yet in my heart, I knew I had said what needed to be said.

Interestingly, the next day that reporter's article came out, and it was written in what a journalist would call perfect inverted-pyramid style, with "just the facts, ma'am." He didn't include his own opinions, nor did he include mine; he stuck with the facts that bore well for BYU.

Fortunately, such moments are rare. And usually in responding to questions from our friends, our colleagues, people we have just met, or even family members, we are not facing a pressing deadline. It is in these cases that I have always found it helpful to slide on the shoes of the other person.

William Eggington, who is a professor in the BYU Department of Linguistics and English Language, gave a BYU devotional in the fall of 2011 in which he talked about the "age of proximity" that we now live in. In this new age, he said, we spend more and more time with people from "other families, other tribes and villages, and other cities, regions, and nations. . . . This situation often threatens to take us out of our same-language and same-cultural comfort zones."[10]

Have you ever tried to explain a green Jell-O joke to someone who has no ties to Utah? They just don't get it. It's not their fault, though. They're certainly not being rude if they don't laugh. Yet sometimes others may view us as self-righteous simply because of the words we have chosen to use. Relationship expert Matt Townsend sat down with Michelle King on *Mormon Times* in December 2011 and shared some ways that we can better communicate the principles of the gospel. With the permission of KSL, let me share with you some of his counsel:

In this program, Matt advises us to share the benefits of living the gospel, not just the lofty principles to which we aspire. Instead of saying, "We don't believe that we should go boating on Sunday because we want to keep the Sabbath day holy," he suggests that we say something others can better understand. Matt explains that keeping the Sabbath day holy is a "beautiful principle, a powerful principle—but behind it others may not have a clue what that means." Yet, he says, there are very real benefits to why we do this. "I teach them the benefits behind it," he explains, "and maybe instead of teaching the principle you can just say, 'You know, we have found family time to be a really important time for our family, and we are trying to get away from doing anything that's really worldly because we found that just getting a time that we're together to hang out and have family time is the only time we have in the week. It brings us closer together.'"

Matt also encourages us to talk with our children about why we live the principles we do. His advice is to talk with our children about our principles—such as believing in paying a full and honest tithe—and what the benefits that we have found in living these principles are. For example, in keeping the Sabbath day holy, what are the values and the benefits behind this principle? "I would have those conversations," Matt says, "so that when people do ask us why we do what we do, we don't come off sounding like we are just quoting the law, but we're quoting the benefit of the law and even our testimony and feelings about it and the why behind it."

Finally, Matt says, "Be real about your values." For instance, he says, if asked to go boating on the Sabbath, we can respond: "It would be so fun to go boating with you on Sunday. We've just made a pact as a family to spend that time together. Let's do it on another day." He concludes, "We can understand why people like to have fun. We can understand why people like to do what they do. We don't need to judge them; we can love them and make things happen."[11]

On Matt's note of letting things happen, particularly once we have put the four Ss in place (our testimony seeps through us, we salute the Savior and His teachings, we are not afraid to speak up, and we slide on the shoes of others), let me conclude with one final piece of counsel I received as a young mother.

After picking up my son and daughter from preschool each day, we always looked for an adventure on the way home. One summer we were really lucky as just a few blocks off our route a beautiful home was being built on a hillside. We would go by this home every single day and study the progress that was being made. Curtis and Lynne especially loved to watch the big trucks driving on and off the property. Finally, on the day the front gates were installed and the house appeared to be finished, I told Curtis and Lynne that we needed to find a new adventure. "But when do we get to go inside the house?" Lynne asked. Completely shocked, I explained to her that I didn't know the owners and that we wouldn't be able to go inside. Without missing a beat, she replied, "Well, Mom, just make friends with them. Then we'll be invited inside."

Of all the ways I know to be a voice for the gospel, they begin with this simple, childlike faith that we can reach across doorsteps, cubicles, and borders to make new friends.

Almost every day I am reminded that the Church is in a special moment right now, where people worldwide are asking, "Who are you?" Doors that I never thought possible are opening, often because of the work of members who live as Emilie, Esther, and Lynne; who explain "who we are and what we believe" by their example, their courage, and their absolute Christlike love; who are, as Elder Ballard says, "honest, open, forthright, engaging, respectful of others' views, and completely nondefensive [of their] own."[12]

It is my hope—for me and for you—that we never let an opportunity pass to be "invited inside." That we heed Paul's counsel to "receive ye one another, as Christ also received us to the glory of God" (Romans 15:7).

NOTES

1. Gordon B. Hinckley, "This Is the Work of the Master," *Ensign*, May 1995, 71.
2. Jamshid Ghazi Askar, "Values-based filmmaker Micheal Flaherty takes the road less traveled," *Deseret News*, 19 November 2011; available at http://www.deseretnews.com/article/700199417/Values-based-filmmaker-Micheal-Flaherty-takes-the-road-less-traveled.html?pg=all; accessed 8 October 2012.
3. Personal correspondence in the author's possession.
4. Hinckley, "The Symbol of Our Faith," *Ensign*, April 2005, 3.
5. Luacine Clark Fox, "Love One Another," *Children's Songbook* (Salt Lake City: The Church of Jesus Christ of Latter-day Saints, 1989), 136.
6. Quentin L. Cook, "We Follow Jesus Christ," *Ensign*, May 2010, 83–86.
7. Ibid.
8. See M. Russell Ballard, "Engaging Without Being Offensive," Summer 2009 commencement address, Brigham Young University, Provo, UT, 19 August 2009; available at http://speeches.byu.edu/index.php?act=viewitem&id=1852; accessed 8 October 2012.
9. Ibid.
10. William Eggington, "Therefore Ye Are No More Strangers and Foreigners," Brigham Young University devotional address, 8 November 2011; available at http://speeches.byu.edu/?act=viewitem&id=2007; accessed 8 October 2012.
11. See *Mormon Times*, 18 December 2011; available at http://www.ksl.com/index.php?nid=1074&sid=18549869&title=december-18-2011; accessed 28 November 2012.
12. Ballard, "Sharing the Gospel with Confidence," *Ensign*, July 2010, 47.

The Power of God in Great Glory!

Elaine S. Dalton and Emi D. Edgley

Elaine: It's so wonderful to be here and to share this time with my daughter, Emi. It's amazing how quickly time passes. It seems like such a short time ago Emi was born; I still remember that day so vividly. This was back when we didn't know if we were having a boy or a girl until the baby was born. Emi is our third child, and I secretly longed for a girl. But when Emi was born, she didn't look like a little girl. I remember she had a little topknot of hair which, as she was born, the doctor promptly cut off and said, "You can't have a curl on this boy!" She's come a long way from that day to this, and her goodness and example tutor me.

It wasn't until after having children that I realized the profound power of covenants in my life. The covenants made at baptism, endowment, and marriage have been significant in my life. I distinctly remember praying as I held each of my children in my arms that they would be

---

Elaine S. Dalton is the Young Women general president. She has served as both first and second counselor in the Young Women general presidency, and on the Young Women general board. She was born and raised in Ogden, Utah. She received her bachelor's degree in English from Brigham Young University. Sister Dalton and her husband, Stephen E. Dalton, are the parents of five sons and one daughter and the grandparents of sixteen grandchildren.

Emi D. Edgley is the daughter of Sister Elaine S. Dalton. She was named the Utah Young Mother of the Year in 2011. She and her husband, Steven, are the parents of two precious daughters.

happy and protected and grow to become all that our Heavenly Father wanted them to become.

Emi: I am grateful to have a mother who honors her covenants and who prays for me, even now that I also am a mother! My mom has always taught, both in word and deed, that family is the most important thing. She loves being a mother. Even within the demands of her calling, she finds time to dance with her granddaughters, orchestrate family gatherings, and share lessons learned from her travels.

My mom and I share a special bond. She has always taught me that I am not only her daughter but also a daughter of God, and as such, Heavenly Father is counting on me to do specific, special, covenant-based work for Him with my life. I remember a letter my mom wrote to me in which she referred to me as a "limited edition of one." Those words—"limited edition of one"—were cemented in my head as I felt, through the Spirit, my identity as a child of God.

My mother and my father have dedicated their lives to covenant relationships that are centered in family life. I have been an eyewitness to my parents trusting God, choosing their actions through the direction and inspiration of the Holy Ghost, and guiding their lives (and in turn, *our* lives) in Christ-centered ways. This has been a great blessing in my life and in the lives of my five brothers.

From my parents, I have learned that I can find power through covenant-centered living. This has been a great strength for me in my marriage and my life as a mother. There are so many loud voices in the world that glorify the secular rather than scriptural, that call for convenience rather than commitment, and that emphasize temporary happiness rather than holiness (see 1 Nephi 8:27–28, 33). My covenants—those that I made at baptism, in the temple, and with my husband, Steve—give me stability as I navigate life's inevitable difficulties and chart my course.

Elaine: Despite all the voices in the world, family is the most important unit in time and eternity, and our covenants provide not only protection and direction but also purpose, peace, and power.

In the Book of Mormon we learn that Nephi saw our day, and he "beheld the power of the Lamb of God, that it descended upon the saints of the church of the Lamb, and upon the covenant people of the Lord, who were scattered upon all the face of the earth; and they were armed with righteousness and with the power of God in great glory" (1 Nephi 14:14). He prophesied that the covenant people would prevail in the latter days. That fact fills me with hope and optimism because I know that whatever storms or difficulties we may encounter, we will be able to prevail as long as we keep our covenants. As members of The Church of Jesus Christ of Latter-day Saints, we are women of covenant, and that knowledge makes us *different*; it makes *all the difference* in our journey through mortality. There is power in making and keeping sacred covenants!

That knowledge refines us, and it defines us. It helps us keep our focus on the things that matter most, and it gives us power to navigate the paths of life. The blessing that was given in Doctrine and Covenants 25 is for each of us as daughters of God. In that blessing we are each told to "walk in the paths of virtue" (D&C 25:2), to "lay aside the things of [the] world, and seek for the things of a better [world]" (D&C 25:10), and to "cleave unto [our] covenants" (D&C 25:13). Making and keeping covenants focuses us on the things that matter most. Our ability to keep our covenants will not only bless us but will be a blessing to generations.

Emi: We come from a long line of noble women who kept their covenants, who were sustained by their covenants, and who were given power to face the challenges of life. Each embraced the Lord's will in her life, and learned to rely on the Lord, despite many hardships. Deaths in their family, particularly those of children or spouses, enhanced their desire to attain exaltation. They put aside troubles and concerns of this world in anticipation of a better. They devoted their lives and all their energy toward the building of the kingdom of God on earth.

They each were sustained and strengthened by their covenants as they faced great difficulties and made many sacrifices. Some of their sacrifices allowed for the building of temples. They understood the need to be armed with righteousness and with the power of God in great glory. Their understanding of the importance of covenants and the accompanying blessings bless my family and me. I now find myself the beneficiary of their being true to their covenants.

Some of you may be the beginning of this line of women who have made and kept their covenants. Your covenants, faithfully observed now, will bless the generations who follow you.

Elaine: When the Saints left Nauvoo and headed west, they suffered unimaginable hardships and privation. What made them do it? What strengthened them for their journey west where they could again build a temple—a house of God? It was their endowment that strengthened them and prepared them for their journey, for they knew that no matter what might happen, the Lord would keep His covenants with them. The temple was central to all because they had made sacred covenants and were endowed with power. Their heartfelt feelings and their knowledge of the power of their covenants are expressed in the hymn "Come, Come, Ye Saints," as they sang, "All is well! All is well!"[1]

Emi: We too are on a journey. We too face opposition and trials and difficulties. We too must know and understand why the early Saints sang "all is well" as they progressed forward in their journey to Zion.

Elaine: What is the source of all moral and spiritual power? This power comes from our Father in Heaven. He is the source of power, and we access that power by making and keeping sacred covenants with Him. What is a covenant? It is an agreement between God and man whose terms are set by God.[2] We enter covenants through priesthood ordinances.

Such was the case of the people in the Book of Mormon who were taught by Alma. They desired with all their hearts to become members of the Savior's Church, and so at the peril of their lives, they gathered at the Waters of Mormon and there at the water's edge, they covenanted to stand as a witness of the Savior "at all times and in all things, and in all places" (Mosiah 18:9) by taking His name upon themselves. They clapped their hands and shouted for joy and exclaimed that this was the desire of their hearts. Later it is recorded that a mighty change of heart occurred, and because of this first covenant, nothing was ever the same. It is recorded, "Yea, the place of Mormon, the waters of Mormon, the forest of Mormon, how beautiful are they to the eyes of them who there came to the knowledge of their Redeemer" (Mosiah 18:30).

BAPTISM

Emi: Our baptism initiates our covenant relationship with God. When we are baptized, we are washed, not only outwardly, but inwardly as well.

The Christmas before our daughter Ella (who is now eleven) was baptized, she requested one gift: a heart-shaped locket. Inside she placed a painting of Jesus and a picture of the temple. She wore this to her baptism, and I am confident that she realized, even at a young age, that her baptism was a first step, a covenant commitment, leading her toward our Savior and the temple.

I thrill with our daughter Louisa, who recently turned seven years old and is counting down the months until her baptism. She cannot wait to follow in the footsteps of Jesus by being obedient. She wants to be cleansed and become a member of The Church of Jesus Christ of Latter-day Saints. I remember those same feelings from when I was baptized—excitement mixed with fear that I might stick my knee or big toe out of the water! And I will never forget the sweet, clean feeling that accompanied my baptism and the bestowal of the gift of the Holy Ghost by my father.

A special part of my baptism day was a gift given to me by my grandma Dalton. She gave me a copy of her baptism memories, which I promptly glued in my new white journal.

My grandmother was baptized almost seventy years prior to me in 1913 at the age of nine. Time and circumstances differentiated her experience from mine, and yet, with the commonality of the gospel ordinances as stepping-stones toward eternal salvation, our shared experiences help to solidify the bonds I feel with her.

She was baptized in a creek rather than a font. Her mother made her a white gown from two sun-bleached flour sacks. The girls undressed behind a clump of wild rose bushes, and the boys (including my grandmother's older brother Clair) undressed behind another clump. When my grandma emerged from the water, traces of lettering on her gown announced the contents to be "Grade A: Four Star."

Elaine: Is not everyone who is baptized with an understanding of the sacred covenants made "Grade A: Four Star?"

Think with me for a moment on the day you were baptized. Do you remember where you were and the people who surrounded you? Do you remember details? Do you remember how you felt and the things you thought? I don't know about you, but even to this day, I remember my baptism as if it were yesterday. I remember details, like the shoes I wore, the feeling I had as I came up out of the water, how it felt to have my father's and grandfathers' hands placed on my head when I was confirmed, and especially the feeling I had when the words "receive the Holy Ghost" were pronounced. I remember telling my cousins at a gathering at our home afterward that I could not play with them any more because somehow we always got in trouble and I was trying to be perfect! I remember never wanting the feeling I had that day to leave me. I was happy, I felt peace, and I felt close to the Savior.

The covenant of baptism is the covenant of salvation. It is a covenant we enter individually—one by one. It is the covenant that opens the door to personal righteousness and power. When a person keeps the baptismal covenant, which is to always remember Him and keep His commandments and endure to the end in faith, then salvation is assured (see 2 Nephi 31; Mosiah 18:8–10).[3]

Emi: This first covenant not only *cleanses* us but *enables* us. And in return for making this covenant, we are promised the companionship of the third member of the Godhead and the power to receive personal revelation for our lives. Thus, in the ordinance of baptism, we are cleansed, and by covenant we agree to keep the commandments and to take upon ourselves the name of Christ, and we promise that we will always walk in the footsteps of the Savior by always remembering Him. When we step out of the waters of baptism, we step out of the world and into the kingdom of our Heavenly Father, and our lives can never really be the same again.[4] That is power!

POWER OF PURITY AND THE HOLY GHOST

Elaine: There is power in purity, and there is power in having the companionship of the Holy Ghost! This is a power that the world does not have nor understand. Those who are baptized are eligible to speak with the tongue of angels and to speak the words of Christ (see 2 Nephi 32:2–3). "The gift of the Holy Ghost comes after one repents and becomes worthy. It is received after baptism by the laying on of hands by those who have the authority."[5] As we live in such a way that we are worthy of the guidance and tutoring of a member of the Godhead, we can go forward confidently because the promise we receive is that the Holy Ghost will "tell you all things what ye should do" (2 Nephi 32:3). And what that means is that we are never alone, and knowing what is right and wrong is always possible. That is power!

Virtue and Purity

Emi: As the Young Women general president, my mom has championed a return to virtue. She lives and teaches that at the very core of power is virtue and that virtue is chastity and moral purity. She has said, "I believe that the disintegration of faith and families . . . [is] directly related to a lack of virtue in our society. And I believe that a return to virtue could save an entire nation."[6]

Elaine: You have heard me talk about the importance of virtue on many occasions and to many different audiences. Why is virtue, meaning moral purity, so important in today's world? Because, simply stated, it is only through virtue and purity that we can receive the companionship of the Holy Ghost. It can be conferred upon us, but we must remain pure, because the Holy Ghost does not dwell in unclean temples—that means in our hearts and in our homes. Is it possible that in these latter days, when temptations and evil surround us and our families, that we do not fully take advantage of this great gift and power? In the world in which we live, is it possible that we make small compromises justifying these on the scale of descending mediocrity by rationalizing that "it is not as bad as . . . ?" The world may be *here* [lower] and we may be *here* [a little bit higher], but we just very well may be heading in the same direction! Thus it is of supreme importance that our homes be places in which the Spirit can dwell. I have discovered, as I am sure you have also, that this takes constant vigilance and work. The Internet, media, and more infiltrate the very walls of our homes. We simply cannot afford as women and mothers to be lured away from our homes or to allow things to enter our homes that will not invite the Spirit to be there. We know this, and yet evil is very patient and waits for a weak moment or a weak spot to manifest itself.

Emi: There is no greater blessing that can come into our lives than to have the Holy Ghost for our constant companion. President James E. Faust once said: "I believe the Spirit of the Holy Ghost is the greatest guarantor of inward peace in our unstable world. It can be more mind-expanding and can make us have a better sense of well-being than any chemical or other earthly substance. It will calm nerves; it will breathe peace to our souls. This Comforter can be with us as we seek to improve. It can function as a source of revelation to warn us of impending danger and also help keep us from making mistakes. It can enhance our natural senses so that we can see more clearly, hear more keenly, and remember what we should remember. It is a way of maximizing our happiness."[7]

Elaine: I agree! That is power! Brigham Young once lamented, "[We] may have the Spirit of the Lord to . . . direct [us]. . . . I am satisfied, however, that in this respect, we live far beneath our privileges."[8]

Why does God require us to make covenants? Covenants are a blessing provided by our Heavenly Father to give us power over evil, deception, and those things that will detract from our happiness as individuals and as families. It is because He loves us and wants us to return to His presence proven, pure, and sealed.

Emi: Integral to returning to His presence pure is our opportunity to personally embrace the redeeming power of the Atonement through the sacrament.

One characteristic of taking the sacrament that gives it great power is that we have the opportunity to partake over and over, for ourselves, week in and week out. About the sacrament, Elder Russell M. Nelson has said: "When we partake of the sacrament, we renew [our baptismal] covenant and declare our willingness to take upon ourselves the name of Jesus Christ. Thereby we are adopted as His sons and daughters and are known as brothers and sisters. He is the father of our new life."[9]

Just as we spoke earlier about the sweet, clean feeling that accompanied our baptisms, the sacrament also holds the power for bringing about a newness of life. President Spencer W. Kimball taught: "*Remembering covenants prevents apostasy*. That is the real purpose of the sacrament, to keep us from forgetting, to help us to remember . . . [that which we have] covenanted at the water's edge or at the sacrament table and in the temple."[10]

There is power in the sacred ordinance of the sacrament! This power is available weekly. Our souls are fed when we partake with a determination to unite our actions with God's. Our paths are made straight when we approach the sacrament with the plea of "more holiness give me,"[11] desiring above all the companionship of His Spirit to be our guide. The eating of the bread and the drinking of water are outward manifestations of our inward, soul-felt desire for renewal and holiness.

I am grateful that partaking of the sacrament is an opportunity that is repeatedly given. Partaking over and over again of the sacrament can assist us in remembering the life of our Savior, remind us of the necessity of repentance and wholehearted devotion to God, and call us to a deeper commitment to life in the covenant.

Endowed with Power

Elaine: As a mother and as the Young Women general president, my vision is the temple. The desire of my heart is to assist parents and priesthood leaders in helping each young woman remain worthy to make and keep sacred covenants and receive the ordinances of the temple. It is in the temple that we are endowed with power from on high. We understand that those who are endowed in the temple are to "be taught from on high" (D&C 43:16). When we receive our temple endowment, which means "gift,"[12] we are "filled with light" and are able to "[comprehend] all things" (D&C 88:67–68). Thus when we receive our endowment in the temple, we also receive the key that unlocks the powers of godliness and the ability to receive knowledge we can obtain in no other way (see D&C 132:18–19). The temple is the reason for everything we do.

Emi: One highlight of my childhood was weekly night rides past the Salt Lake Temple. In an effort to prepare us for bedtime and perhaps just to keep us contained and off our usual paths of destruction, we would pile into the family Pinto and head downtown.

On those nights, we would watch for the illuminated spires of the temple, and my older brothers, always first to see the building, would shout, "The temple, the temple!" My mom would ask each of us, "Where do you want to get married?" When she asked, "Emi, where do you want to get married?" I always responded, "The temple!"

Night rides, walks around the temple grounds, and watching my parents prepare to attend the temple on their date night all provided simple preparation in the form of exposure to the value of covenants.

Elaine: I don't think I will ever forget the day when I went to the temple to receive my own endowments. My mother tried to prepare me as best she could on the ride from Ogden to the Salt Lake Temple. She explained to me that in the temple there was a lot of symbolism, that I would not understand everything the first visit, and would want to return to the temple often to gain more understanding. I didn't know what to expect. But when I came out of the temple that evening, I was filled with joy. My mother asked me how I felt, and I told her that everything I had ever wanted was given to me that day in the house of the Lord. And it was.

Emi: I feel like, with life experience, I continue to unfold layer upon layer of the value of covenants.[13] Why do we make covenants? Why are we a covenant people? It is because these covenants give us power, protection, peace of mind, and even confidence as we journey through life. With the backing of covenants, we can embark upon uncharted territory with a confidence that affects how we deal with the challenges of life.

When Steve and I were married, I felt so grateful to be sealed and to pledge our love and loyalty for time and all eternity. Yet I gained a new perspective on the sealing covenant that binds Steve and me and our children when our first daughter was stillborn. Years before, I felt like I understood the impact of eternal marriage, of our hearts being turned to our fathers, and of our children sealed to us through the sacred ordinances of the temple. Now I understand this more. As a family, we have both the motivation as well as the solace that comes of knowing that, if we live worthily, we can be together in the eternities. Peace comes from the promise of being together.

Elaine: When we attend the temple, the Lord promises each of us that we will come forth from His holy house "endowed with power from on high" (D&C 38:32). We will receive protection from heavenly hosts and "angels [shall have] charge concerning [us]" (Matthew 4:6). This means that we need never face the adversary alone. It means we never have to go through trials, discouragements, or disappointments alone. The promise given from the Lord assures each of us that "I will go before your face. I will be on your right hand and on your left, and my Spirit shall be in your hearts, and mine angels round about you, to bear you up" (D&C 84:88).

These are the promises to the Lord's covenant people—the house of Israel. I testify that they are true and that they apply here and now and not to some distant future. As the Prophet Joseph Smith dedicated the Kirtland Temple, he prayed that we might have the power of the covenants. Listen to these beautiful words and promises in the dedicatory prayer of the Kirtland Temple: "We ask thee, Holy Father, that thy servants may go forth from this house armed with thy power, and that thy name may be upon them, and thy glory be round about them, and thine angels have charge over them; . . . That no weapon formed against them shall prosper; . . . And if any people shall rise against this people, that thine anger be kindled against them; And if they shall smite this people thou wilt smite them; thou wilt fight for thy people . . . that they may be delivered from the hands of all their enemies" (D&C 109:22, 25, 27–28).

Eternal Marriage

An integral part of the new and everlasting covenant, which is the restored gospel of Jesus Christ, is the covenant of celestial marriage—the covenant of exaltation. When we are sealed in the temple, ultimately we may become joint heirs to the blessings of the Abrahamic covenant, some of which include an eternal family and the blessings of power and glory and exaltation (see D&C 132:19–20.) Through the covenant of celestial marriage we become joint heirs to all the blessings promised to Abraham, Isaac, and Jacob if we are faithful.[14] I will never forget the day my husband, Steve, and I knelt across the altar from each other and looked into each other's eyes. As I knelt in the temple that day, dressed in white, I heard words and made covenants that thrilled me. I felt a powerful connection with the eternities. At the time, I didn't fully comprehend, however, what those covenants meant or would mean in my life, but upon returning to the temple in subsequent years, I grew in my understanding as I witnessed other marriages and sealings. When I entered the temple and saw our sons and our daughter, Emi, dressed in white, kneeling at that same altar, making those same covenants, I understood more clearly what covenants really mean in this journey through mortality. And as your mother, Emi, I was so grateful that you had lived your life in such a way that you would now be given the protection, the power, and the promise associated with making and keeping sacred covenants.

The Savior is the center of a covenant marriage in the temple. Elder David A. Bednar taught that as a husband and wife individually draw closer to the Savior, they also come closer together in their marriage relationship.[15] The covenants we make are not restrictive, as some might suppose, but are actually enabling and expanding. They make us free to receive more and more of the blessings that our Father has in store to bestow upon us. Our covenants are like armor. Our Heavenly Father has prepared them for us to protect us and defend us against evil.

Emi: My parents would often talk with us about their wedding day—the day they were sealed for time and all eternity. My dad still jokes about the work he had to do to convince Mom to marry him and the associated heel marks that he claims are still on the sidewalk to this day outside the temple where he dragged my mom inside on that Friday the thirteenth wedding day so many years ago. Mom, you and Dad sure have come a long way from the heel marks!

Elaine: Well, I did get a little nervous at the last minute. But we didn't have any problem getting a time at the temple. No one else was there, and Friday the thirteenth is now our lucky day!

Now I am experiencing another wonderful blessing. My husband, Steve, is a sealer in the Salt Lake Temple. There is no greater power on the earth. Each time I attend a wedding or go to the temple to do sealings for our ancestors, I am overcome with a realization of the eternal blessings of covenants found in the temple. As I see my husband dressed in white performing these sacred ordinances, I hear the covenant blessings in an entirely different way.

Emi: I learned on the day *my* Steve and I were married in the Salt Lake Temple (yes, I also married a Steve!) the key to the visions of eternity—of generations linked both forward and backward in time. And I learned this by looking through the reflective glass of temple mirrors. As Steve and I knelt at the altar, if I focused my sights on myself (or my hair, which I was particularly concerned about that day), I was able to see only the two of us and our immediate surroundings. Yet as I focused on the mirrors and the reflections, I could see that the generations that preceded us and the generations that followed would be impacted by our choices.

Another temple experience occurred when I was able to attend the dedication of the Jordan River Utah Temple as an eight-year-old. I had seen the amazing architecture of many temples but was mostly intrigued with all I had heard about the beautiful interiors, complete with sparkly chandeliers and reflective mirrors. Yet on this special day when I was seated with my family, I found myself in an area composed completely of exposed concrete. I think I took part in the dedication from the confines of the temple parking garage! I saw nothing special, yet still felt the Spirit and the significance of a temple dedicated to the Lord's work.

Similarly, my daughter Ella had the opportunity, at the age of eight, to attend the Draper Utah Temple dedication. Unlike my experience in the parking garage, she was seated in a light-filled room with sparkling chandeliers and mirrors. Of this experience she wrote, "I want to remember this moment. During the dedication, I could hear more than I could see; meaning there was only a choir of thirty, but I could hear thousands singing beautifully. I could really feel the Spirit. Today I learned that temples always are peaceful places and the Spirit of God can come and attend with us."[16]

Elaine: The Prophet Joseph Smith taught that the divine purpose of God is to gather his people so that they can build temples and receive the highest ordinances and gain eternal life.[17] In the Book of Mormon we learn of the latter days. Elder Neal A. Maxwell explained that "when we baptize, our eyes should gaze beyond the baptismal font to the holy temple. The great garner into which the sheaves should be gathered is the holy temple."[18] The temple thus becomes a refuge and a protection to all who are worthy to enter these sacred doors.

In the Young Women auxiliary, Personal Progress helps a young woman focus on and prepare for the ordinances of the temple. Mothers, you would be wise to assist your daughters with this preparation. Your love of your daughter and your eternal bonds will be increased as you study scriptures together and learn doctrines and principles that will strengthen your home and your family. And the eternal bonds you share will be strengthened.

I recently found one of Emi's old Personal Progress books. It was a sweet experience for me to read her goals and to now realize how those small and simple commitments she made then formed and molded her testimony and her desire to make and keep sacred covenants.

Emi: Personal Progress really helped me to stay on the right track. From Personal Progress and the Young Women program, I learned about making commitments—commitments to family, friends, and myself as well as commitments to my Heavenly Father. Goals made in Personal Progress encouraged me to pray, to be protected, and to read my scriptures, which brought the guidance of the Spirit into my life and prepared me to remain pure and worthy to enter the temple. Those choices help to remind us as women and young women about our baptismal covenants, and to refine and prepare us to return to our heavenly home.

Elaine: Now with all this talk of the power of covenants and covenant making, I know there are those here today whose hearts are broken because covenants have been broken. You may not have a perfect family. Neither do we. But we are striving and trying and seeking after righteousness. We know that we cannot force others to keep their covenants, but we can keep ours. The power of your covenant and worthy life will pull down blessings on you and on your wayward children. Your covenants will help you know what to say and what to do. The Prophet Joseph Smith plainly taught, "When a seal is put upon the father and mother, it secures their posterity so that they cannot be lost, but will be saved by virtue of the covenant of their father and mother."[19] "Covenants remembered by parents will be remembered by God."[20]

As Elder Jeffrey R. Holland so beautifully taught in April general conference, I now repeat here to you: "So if you have made covenants, keep them. If you haven't made them, make them. If you have made them and broken them, repent and repair them. It is *never* too late so long as the Master of the vineyard says there is time."[21] Elder M. Russell Ballard said it best when he said: "Every sister who stands for truth and righteousness diminishes the influence of evil. Every sister who strengthens and protects her family is doing the work of God. Every sister who lives as a woman of God becomes a beacon for others to follow and plants seeds of righteous influence that will be harvested for decades to come. Every sister who makes and keeps sacred covenants becomes an instrument in the hands of God."[22] That is power. That is our power.

Emi: Every gospel ordinance—every covenant made—focuses on the Atonement of Jesus Christ. Last year my family and I attended the Carl Bloch art exhibit, *The Master's Hand,* at Brigham Young University's Museum of Art. As we entered the gallery, there was a hushed reverence and a feeling as if we were in the presence of greatness. Through the artist's magnificent work, we could feel the Spirit of the great individual portrayed, that of Jesus Christ.

The first painting we viewed was *The Doubting Thomas.* Rather than depicting Thomas's act of touching the resurrected Savior's wounds, Bloch captures the moment when Thomas first recognized Jesus as his personal Redeemer.

We were among a crowd and stood at a respectful distance. Yet my daughter Ella, compelled by the image, separated herself from the crowd to closely approach the Savior as depicted in the larger-than-life mural. I watched as she studied the Savior. I marveled at how children are so close to the Savior; they often set the example and show us the way we should be. I grew in my appreciation of the Savior, whose sacrifice unleashed the power of the Atonement and the Resurrection.

Making and keeping covenants provides opportunities for me—for each of us—to approach the Savior. Our Savior, Jesus Christ, stands preeminent in my life. I hope to reflect His light, to be armed with the power of God in great glory, and to emulate His life through the soul-refining process of making and keeping sacred covenants.

Let me share with you a true story. A friend of ours was on a humanitarian trip to build new classrooms in rural South America. While he was flying to a remote Guatemalan village in a single-engine plane, the engine died. All fourteen passengers aboard knew that a crash landing on the dense jungle floor below was imminent. For minutes there was silence and an eerie calm as the plane glided and lost altitude. Our friend was left to his thoughts about his family and his life. He and those aboard braced themselves for the inevitable, and in his mind, he realized, *I am going to die.* His next thought was, *It's okay.* He turned to his coworker, friend, and seatmate, and his friend's last words were, "If it's our time, it's our time." He nodded in agreement and then thought to himself, "I have kept my covenants." The plane crashed. Eleven of the fourteen aboard did not survive. Our friend—badly injured—was pulled by men working in the fields nearby from the wreckage just before the plane burst into flames.

His life in the years that have passed has been shaped by this experience. He still suffers effects of the injuries sustained on that day, and yet he moves forward with a renewed power and an enhanced perspective of the grand experience of earth life. This is the kind of confidence we can carry into daily decisions when our choices are accompanied with the most important declaration that can be made: "I have made and kept sacred covenants."

It is my prayer that each of us will leave today with this determination: "And this shall be our covenant—that we will walk in all the ordinances of the Lord" (D&C 136:4).

Elaine: The greatest compliment that can come to us in this life is to be known as a covenant keeper. It was said of a group of valiant young men in the Book of Mormon that "they were . . . true at all times in whatsoever thing they were entrusted" (Alma 53:20). They kept their covenants. May it also be recorded that each of us kept our covenants.

Now Emi and I and Ella and Louisa join that long line of women that cherished and cleaved to their covenants. My mother Emma is now ninety-one years old. Half of those ninety-one years she has lived as a widow. Emi was named after her. Today we would like to pay her the ultimate compliment—she is a covenant keeper.

Our family motto simply states—*We will be true*. It is my prayer for my family and for each of us here today that our lives will be centered on the Savior and keeping our covenants.

I am grateful for a Savior and the redeeming and enabling power of His infinite atoning sacrifice. I am grateful that He was true at all times and in all things and in all places and for the example He set as He marked the path and led the way. I am grateful for His light and life. I am grateful for the blessings I receive because He kept His premortal covenants with the Father. I shall ever owe to Him my gratitude, my love, and my life. Today, we testify that He lives!

NOTES

1. William W. Phelps, "Come, Come, Ye Saints," *Hymns of The Church of Jesus Christ of Latter-day Saints* (Salt Lake City: The Church of Jesus Christ of Latter-day Saints, 1985), no. 30.
2. See Bible Dictionary, s.v., "Covenant," 651.
3. See also Bruce R. McConkie, *Mormon Doctrine*, 2nd ed. (Salt Lake City: Bookcraft, 1966), 166–68.
4. See Robert D. Hales, *Return* (Salt Lake City: Deseret Book, 2010), 60.
5. James E. Faust, "The Gift of the Holy Ghost—A Sure Compass," *Ensign*, April 1996, 4.
6. Elaine S. Dalton, "Zion Is the Pure in Heart," in *Church News*, 13 September 2009; available at http://www.ldschurchnews.com/articles/58277/Elaine-S-Dalton-Zion-Is-the-Pure-in-Heart.html; accessed 15 October 2012.
7. Faust, "The Gift of the Holy Ghost—A Sure Compass," 5.
8. Brigham Young, *Discourses of Brigham Young*, Compiled by John A. Widtsoe (Salt Lake City: Deseret Book, 1973), 32.
9. Russell M. Nelson, "Covenants," *Ensign*, November 2011, 88.
10. Spencer W. Kimball, *The Teachings of Spencer W. Kimball*, ed. Edward L. Kimball (Salt Lake City: Bookcraft, 1982), 112.
11. Philip Paul Bliss, "More Holiness Give Me," *Hymns*, no. 131.
12. See Hales, "Blessings of the Temple," *Ensign*, October 2009, 46–49.
13. See Richard G. Scott, "The Eternal Blessings of Marriage," *Ensign*, May 2011, 84–97.
14. See Russell M. Nelson, *Ensign*, "Covenants," November 2011, 86–89.
15. See David A. Bednar, "Marriage Is Essential to His Eternal Plan," *Worldwide Leadership Training Meeting*, 11 February 2006, 2–7.
16. Personal correspondence in author's possession.
17. See Joseph Smith, *Joseph Smith*, in Teaching of Presidents of the Church series (Salt Lake City: The Church of Jesus Christ of Latter-day Saints, 2007), 415–17.
18. Neal A. Maxwell, in John L. Hart, "Make Calling Focus of Your Mission," *Church News*, 17 September 1994, 4.
19. *History of The Church of Jesus Christ of Latter-day Saints*, 7 vols., ed. B. H. Roberts (Salt Lake City: The Church of Jesus Christ of Latter-day Saints, 1932–51), 5:530.
20. Faust, "The Greatest Challenge in the World—Good Parenting," *Ensign*, November 1990, 35.
21. Jeffrey R. Holland, "The Laborers in the Vineyard," *Ensign*, May 2012, 33.
22. M. Russell Ballard, "Women of Righteousness," *Ensign*, April 2002, 70.

Mormon's Warning: Arming Your Home and Family

Chad Lewis

I was taught by loving parents and wise mission presidents that there is a principle of life that I would do well to obey. They called it "marrying up." I was obedient to their counsel, and it has made all the difference. Michele is my best friend, and I am honored to be her husband and stand with her today.

In January of 2005, the Philadelphia Eagles were playing in our fourth consecutive NFC Championship game. That sounds pretty sweet if you are an Eagles fan. But we had lost the first three against the Saint Louis Rams, the Tampa Bay Buccaneers, and finally the Carolina Panthers. Each loss was more devastating than the previous one.

Thankfully, we were led by an indomitable coach named Andy Reid. He helped us stay mentally strong and push each other to return to the championship game for the fourth year in a row.

That fourth game against the Atlanta Falcons was played on a freezing cold Philadelphia winter evening with a foot of snow on the ground. As the starting tight end, I almost did not get a chance to play in that game because of a triceps injury I received in the playoff game the week

---

Chad Lewis received his bachelor's degree in communication studies from Brigham Young University. He was a four-year starter and Academic All-American on the football team, and went on to become a three-time Pro-Bowl player for the NFL with the Philadelphia Eagles. He is an associate athletic director for development at BYU. He served a mission in Taiwan, and serves as a stake high councilor. He and his wife, Michele, are the parents of seven children.

before. I got as much treatment as I could from my trainers in the week leading up to the big game. The Eagles did everything they could to help me get back on the field.

But there was something more to be done. I asked my dad to give me a priesthood blessing when he flew out for the game. It was something he had done many times before.

Just a few hours before the biggest game of my life, I was surrounded by my family in a hotel room next to the stadium. My dad and two brothers put their hands on my head and gave me a priesthood blessing. The feeling I felt was one of peace and comfort. I am sure that you know just the feeling I am describing. With the pressure of the game on my shoulders, it was nice to feel that feeling. It was a miracle.

The game went better than I could have dreamed. I caught two touchdowns to help our team beat the Falcons and earn a spot in Super Bowl XXXIX, something I will never forget.

But before I tell you why I did not play one down in the Super Bowl, I need to explain what happened when I caught my second touchdown pass. I twisted to catch a pass in the corner of the end zone, and my left foot exploded. As I was falling to the ground, holding the football tight in my arms, time seemed to stop, and the rush and speed of the game stood still.

I remember very clearly thinking that we were going to the Super Bowl. At the same time, I also knew that I would not be playing. Immediately, there came a feeling into my mind that I can only describe as divine. It was the exact same feeling I had when my dad was giving me a blessing. I felt peace and comfort. I knew that everything was as it should be.

I remained seated as I celebrated the touchdown. When the other tight end helped me up, I told him that I'd broken my foot. What actually happened was that I had torn the Lisfranc ligament in my foot. That is the key ligament which holds my foot together from top to bottom and from side to side. It was the most exciting, disappointing moment of my life.

X-rays in the locker room concluded that I had positively torn my Lisfranc and that I would not be playing in the Super Bowl. After the X-rays were taken, we huddled as a family in an exam room in the training room. Again, hands were laid on my head, and again I was blessed by my dad and brothers with a priesthood blessing. And once again I had feelings of peace and comfort. Even in the midst of disappointment and frustration, there was peace and strength, there was love. My parents and my family brought me to the divine peace of the Savior.

Some may wonder why I received such a severe injury when I had just barely been given a priesthood blessing before the game. I came away from that experience understanding that a testimony of God and the living Christ was much more important than physical health.

Don't ever hesitate to ask for a blessing. It might be the best thing for both you and the person who is giving the blessing. Priesthood blessings are one of the great tools the Savior gives us to protect our families.

Michele and I have thought long and hard about you, and about the topic of our presentation: "Mormon's Warning: Arming Your Home and Family." What do we learn from the Book of Mormon about this?

The Nephites prepared countless times for possible attacks, both expected and unknown. Captain Moroni helped the Nephites stay one step ahead of the Lamanites because he sought the inspiration of heaven to defend his people.

In Alma 49, it says: "But behold, to their uttermost astonishment, they were prepared for them, in a manner which never had been known among the children of Lehi. Now they were prepared for the Lamanites, to battle after the manner of the instructions of Moroni. And it came to pass that the Lamanites, or the Amalickiahites, were exceedingly astonished at their manner of preparation for war" (Alma 49:8–9). I love that description! How can we be like the Nephites and protect our homes and families?

Moroni made their weak places strong. He had a ditch dug around their cities with a high bank of earth thrown up and also walls of stone to protect them. He had their bodies covered in armor with shields, breastplates, and headplates. What spiritual and temporal tools and defenses can we fashion to prepare our "young people [who] are being raised in enemy territory"?[1]

Like the Nephites, we have been prepared after the manner of living prophets. And when we are obedient to the counsel of our prophets and apostles, we will be blessed and protected. Our homes will be strong.

The greatest defense in the universe is the gospel of Jesus Christ, His Atonement, His love, His protection, His wisdom and peace. As parents we can help our children find their way to the Savior's presence. We can guide them to real safety. We can love and encourage them when they feel awkward and unworthy. We can even carry them when they lose strength or hope or faith. We can lovingly ask them tough questions about morality and about their surroundings in school. We can have the courage to tell them no when the Spirit urges us to do so, even when we feel peer pressure to go along with the crowd.

When Elder Patrick Kearon spoke in the priesthood session of general conference in October 2010, he shared an invitation from the Savior to the Nephites which touched my heart. Elder Ronald Rasband also quoted the same verse in the April 2012 general conference.[2]

Listen as the Savior invites parents to bring our children to Him. This word *bring* is one of the tools we can use to astonish the adversary. It takes love, the Savior's love—something the adversary doesn't understand.

"Our Savior is the Prince of Peace, the Great Healer, the only One who can truly cleanse us from the sting of sin and the poison of pride and change our rebellious hearts into converted, covenant hearts. His Atonement is infinite and embraces us all.

"The invitation given to the Nephites, when He ministered to them as the resurrected Christ, is still in force for you and for me: 'Have ye any that are sick among you? Bring them hither. Have ye any that are lame, or blind, or halt, or maimed, or leprous, or that are withered, or that are deaf, or that are afflicted in any manner? Bring them hither *and I will heal them*' (3 Nephi 17:7; emphasis added)."[3]

"Bring them hither"—that is the invitation. Bring them to Christ. How can we do it?

Let our homes ring with great music that will bring our children to Christ. If we don't help our children know what great music is, who will? If we don't help them learn to have an appetite for inspiring and uplifting music, I guarantee the enemy to their souls will have no problem stealing their peace and replacing it with evil words and rhythms and beats and lyrics—the only music available in the great and spacious building.

There are highly intelligent individuals in this world who are laboring and scheming in the boardrooms of companies and organizations who have money and marketing power and appeal and who will stop at nothing to surround our children with their filthy music and their wicked images. They will do anything to make their message look cool and sound hip.

Our children are counting on us to help them find the way. They are counting on us to lead them and guide them and to walk beside them. They are counting on us.

The lines of right and wrong are purposely made blurry by the evil one. Of our time, President Boyd K. Packer has said, "I know of nothing in the history of the Church or in the history of the world to compare with our present circumstances. Nothing happened in Sodom and Gomorrah which exceeds the wickedness and depravity which surrounds us now."[4]

Women's Conference is the perfect setting to share what President Heber J. Grant said about LDS mothers in the middle of these important times: "Without the devotion and absolute testimony of the living God in the hearts of our mothers, this Church would die."[5] You are strong. Strong enough to bring those you love to the feet of the Savior.

My mom did that for me twenty-two years ago as I was preparing for my mission. Four months before I went to Taiwan, my dad suffered a massive stroke. It happened on the night of July 2. Before my dad was taken to the hospital, he was given a priesthood blessing by my brother Jason, who had just returned from his mission to Argentina, as well as our home teacher, Larry Heaps.

Once we got to the emergency room, it was obvious that my dad's condition was life-threatening. He was given an MRI to accurately diagnose the source of the extreme pain coming from his head. The image from the MRI showed he had an aneurysm that would kill him unless the clot could be removed and the bleeding stopped.

He was rushed into surgery. We found a room where we could be alone, and my mom asked Larry Heaps to offer a prayer for my family and for my dad. I remember kneeling on the ground—it was hard—and crying as Larry prayed for all of us. I felt almost too weak to walk, but there he was, helping us into the presence of the Savior.

My mom knew that was what we needed. That was how she was

raised by her parents. After a lifetime of them bringing her to the Savior, she was doing the same thing for our family. The doctor told us that the chance of my dad surviving surgery did not look good.

Our prayers were answered, though, and my dad's life was spared. The surgery was serious enough that we were told he would never move his left side again. Over the next two months that he stayed in the hospital, we witnessed miracles, both small and great. Not only did he regain the ability to walk, but as a family we found the love and grace of God in the middle of our tribulations. We loved and cherished one another more than we ever had before. We discovered what Victor Hugo meant in his Christian story of *Les Miserables*, that "to love another person is to see the face of God."[6]

In those delicate and trying days after my dad's stroke, my mom taught us the lesson shared by President Thomas S. Monson; it was important that we think to thank, and pause to pray.[7]

She went to the gift shop of the hospital and purchased a small journal, which she called our blessings book. We gathered together as a family for prayer each night and we would write in our blessings book everything we were thankful for. Instead of dwelling on things we didn't have, she helped us focus on things that we did have.

My parents taught me that prayer was more important than money and faith more powerful than the cords of death.

My parents taught me the power of great music as my dad listened to his favorite tape of Beethoven's Ninth Symphony, the *Ode to Joy*, over and over again in his hospital room. That music helped create an atmosphere where miracles could take place. He was surrounded by great music.

My parents had armed our home and family with the gospel of Jesus Christ. During those two months, we fasted and prayed. Our neighbors, friends, and ward members fasted and prayed with us and for us. We gathered in the hospital each night for family prayer, and we were given the strength to move forward for another day.

It was a miracle to each one of us who were involved in his healing process. I received and opened my mission call in his hospital room. I couldn't wait to get to Taiwan and let the people know about the restoration of the priesthood that had just saved my dad's life and helped him return to health.

Being a missionary changed my life. As I worked to bring my Chinese brothers and sisters to Christ, I found that they brought me closer to Christ. My mission presidents, Kent Watson and Tim Stratford, tutored me and encouraged me with wisdom to follow the Savior. So did my companions. That was the Lord's university. It is available to every young man and woman in the Church.

When I was playing for the Eagles, Paul Tagliabue, the commissioner of the National Football League, asked me to be an ambassador for the NFL in China. I knew I wasn't the smartest player in the NFL, but I was the *only* one who could speak Mandarin Chinese.

One of my first assignments was to cover the Super Bowl in Chinese for the first live broadcast to China. I was thrilled, but then I realized I did not know how to say *quarterback* in Chinese. That could be a real problem. Sure I could speak Chinese, but I was limited to speaking missionary Chinese. I had no problem teaching about the Atonement, but how was I going to describe the game without knowing any of the vocabulary?

I called the league office the following day and let them know that I was probably not the best fit to be in the television booth. They just told me I would be fine. I told them to hang on. "You'll get what you get and you won't throw a fit."

I studied my old missionary language materials and prepared the best that I could. It was not a surprise to me but it may have been to others that in describing plays on the field, I testified that Tom Brady was throwing true passes.

When my Chinese broadcast partner made a big deal out of the fact that I had four children at the time, I responded to him, "*Shr Jye Shang Mei You Cheng Gung Neng Ni Bu Jya Ting de Shr Bai*," which means, "No success in the world can compensate for failure in the home."

The NFL has given me many opportunities around the world to share my love of football. Last year I was asked to hike Mount Kilimanjaro with Jeff Fisher, the head coach of the St. Louis Rams, and Tedy Bruschi, a three-time Super Bowl champion and middle linebacker for the New England Patriots.

We were asked to accompany four wounded warriors from our nation's military who had not long before been injured in Iraq and Afghanistan. Two of the warriors had their right legs amputated below the knee as a result of IED blasts, one suffered from severe post-traumatic stress disorder, and the other had had her right eye blown out.

The summit of Mount Kilimanjaro is 19,341 feet. The hike would take us five days up and two days to get back down. Our guide, Nickson Moshi, had been to the summit over five hundred times. When he spoke, we listened. He told us that above eighteen thousand feet was considered the danger zone, and our lives depended on trusting his words and commands.

The scenery was majestic, and the views above the clouds were breathtaking. We were there to help shine the spotlight on the Wounded Warrior Project, which helps our veterans return from war with their injuries, both seen and unseen, and get back into life and get into school and find jobs. As we climbed, we spoke with the warriors and learned of their incredible experiences in war. The statement of standing in harm's way for our freedom took on a whole new meaning for us.

There were hilarious moments, like when Bryan Wagner would step in freezing cold mountain runoff water with his titanium leg and tell us how cold it was.

The higher up the mountain we climbed, the more tired we all felt. Our goal was to help all of the warriors stand on the summit. That goal was not to be realized, as two of the warriors started to experience some real problems.

The first was Ben Lunak. His stump started to deteriorate. It was swollen and painful, and the skin was wearing against his prosthetic leg and breaking down. The day before we would summit, Ben let us know that he would not be able to finish the climb. He was escorted to a stretcher and carried back down the mountain by the porters who were there to help us carry all of our gear.

One of the best parts of the expedition was when Tedy Bruschi pulled Ben aside just before he was put on the stretcher. Tedy let Ben know how proud of him we all were. And then he told Ben that a part of him was going to the summit after all. Tedy asked Ben to give him his leg! Tedy put Ben's leg into his backpack and charged up the mountain.

After another full day of hiking, we had dinner and then rested for a couple of hours, and then hiked through the night for the summit. It was the steepest and most difficult part of the entire trip.

When we were within two thousand feet of the summit, another one of the warriors had a problem. Michael Wilson, a Marine from Maryland, started vomiting like crazy. We waited on the trail for him to get better, but it never happened. Altitude sickness hit Michael very hard. One of our guides told Michael that if he tried to go any higher, he would lose his life. In tears, he trusted the guide and headed back down the mountain.

The rest of our group continued on up the mountain. When we were getting close to the summit, Tedy let me know that he was exhausted and asked if I would help him carry Ben's leg. I felt bad that Tedy had carried it the whole way, and I grabbed the leg and threw it in my backpack. Then the sun rose over Africa. After hiking all night, it was a glorious sight to see.

Photo courtesy Chad Lewis.

Team Hard Target, representing the Wounded Warriors Project and the NFL, at the summit of Mt. Kilimanjaro. From left to right, Tedy Bruschi, David Krichavsky, John Sullivan, Bryan Wagner, Nancy Schilliro, Chad Lewis, and Jeff Fisher, who is holding Ben Lunak's leg, which Tedy Bruschi and Chad Lewis carried to the summit.

As a group, we finally made it to the summit of Mount Kilimanjaro. It was a triumphant moment to take a picture and wave our banners at the top of the mountain. Notice Jeff Fisher holding Ben's leg in this photo at the top. And, of course, I had to represent for BYU on the roof of Africa!

Since we did not have supplemental oxygen, we all had terrible headaches. I have never had a headache like that before, even after getting smashed in football games. It was altogether different, and it was a reminder that we were in the danger zone. I couldn't wait to get back down where the air was full of oxygen and we would be out of harm's way.

But I had one more banner to wave. Sister Elaine S. Dalton, the general president of the Young Women auxiliary, had given me a gold banner of virtue to wave at the summit. Virtue is another powerful tool to help arm our home and family in these last days. I had had my family sign this banner before I left for the trip. And when I pulled it out, I thought of them and shouted, "Hurrah for Israel!" All the people on Team Hard Target thought I was crazy.

Families are forever and they are worth fighting for. They are worth doing whatever we can to arm them with righteousness for the battles that surround us.

We had a long, long way to go to get down. At that elevation, my strength was almost gone. It was difficult to catch my breath. I had a guide named Damian that hiked down with me. He noticed that I was getting very tired and asked me if he could carry my backpack.

I told him that I was carrying Ben's leg and that I needed to do it myself. Even though I was so tired that I was ready to tip over and collapse, I had too much pride to let Damian help me to safety.

About fifteen seconds later, Damian said, "Chad, let me carry your backpack. My job is to help you get back to camp safely. I am not tired at all. I do this every week. The altitude does not bother me one bit. Please let me carry your backpack and help you get back to camp safely."

In desperation and exhaustion, I gave my backpack to Damian. Why was I so stubborn that I resisted his help at first? Why did I have so much pride that I was ready to tip over and faint before I let him help me?

As I was walking down, I thought of the Savior standing with open arms, waiting for me to go to Him. I thought of my own pride and the times when I have been slow to hear Him. I thought of His Atonement, and His invitation to cast my burdens at His feet. His loving kindness was overpowering. What I wanted more than anything was His peace and love and mercy. As soon as we were back in camp, I gave Damian a great big hug, and I told him how much I loved him for helping me get back to my family in one piece.

Our whole team made it down the mountain. We were exhausted. It took us two days to hike all the way down to the bottom. Michael Wilson required a stretcher to get down because his condition had gotten worse since he had thrown up so much on the trail.

An amazing thing happened once we finally got to the bottom. Our headaches disappeared. Even Michael felt great. In fact, he wanted to eat some pizza. That surprised me—I thought he was going to be sent to the emergency room for sure. But once he was out of danger, once he was back to safety, with air that was full of oxygen, he felt better than before. He was more grateful than ever for his health, and his life.

The Savior is our defense. He is our peace. Jesus Christ is our Redeemer. He is worth any sacrifice to be obedient to His commandments. His tools of prayers, scripture study, fasting, faith, priesthood blessings, great music, and love, will help us return to Him. As parents, we should remember His invitation to "bring them hither that I may heal them."

NOTES

1. Boyd K. Packer, "Counsel to Youth," *Ensign*, November 2011, 16.
2. See Ronald A. Rasband, "Special Lessons," *Ensign*, May 2012, 80–82, note 3.
3. Patrick Kearon, "'Come unto Me with Full Purpose of Heart, and I Shall Heal You,'" *Ensign*, November 2010, 52.
4. Packer, address to Church Educational System religious educators, 6 February 2004, in *Religious Educator* 5, no. 2 (2004): 1–11; available at http://rsc.byu.edu/archived/voice-my-servants-apostolic-messages-teaching-learning-and-scripture/one-pure-defense-0; accessed 9 October 2012.
5. Heber J. Grant, *Gospel Standards*, comp. G. Homer Durham (Salt Lake City: The Improvement Era, 1941), 151.
6. See http://www.brainyquote.com/quotes/quotes/v/victorhugo152557.html; accessed 9 October 2012.
7. See Thomas S. Monson, "Success Steps to the Abundant Life," *New Era*, May 1971, 2.

Patience: A Gift of the Spirit, a Divine Attribute

Mary Ellen Edmunds

President Dieter F. Uchtdorf, in the 2011 general Relief Society meeting, said, "You are closer to heaven than you suppose."[1] I'll start with a story that most of you have heard before, but I think it will set the stage for what I'd like to share:

It's a story about a woman who had the patience of a saint. A man observed her in the grocery store with a little girl in her cart. As they passed the cookie section, the child asked for cookies and her mother told her no. The little girl immediately began to whine and fuss, and the mother said quietly, "Now, Ella, we just have half of the aisles left to go through. Don't be upset. It won't be long."

The man passed the mother again in the candy aisle. Of course, the little girl began to shout for candy. When she was told she couldn't have any, she began to cry. The mother said, "There, there, Ella, don't cry. Only two more aisles to go, and then we'll be checking out."

The man again happened to be behind the pair at the checkout, where the little girl immediately began to clamor for gum and burst into a terrible tantrum upon discovering there would be no gum purchased today.

Mary Ellen Edmunds is the author of, among other books, Buck Up, Little Buckaroo *and* Peculiar—in a Good Way. *Trained as a nurse, she is also the former director of training for the Provo Missionary Training Center and a former member of the Relief Society general board.*

The mother patiently said, "Ella, we'll be through this checkout stand in five minutes, and then you can go home and have a nice nap."

The man followed them out to the parking lot and stopped the woman to compliment her. "I couldn't help noticing how patient you were with little Ella . . ."

The mother broke in—"My little girl's name is Kaitlyn. *I'm* Ella."

DO YOU EVER GET IMPATIENT WITH YOURSELF?

If you're normal, you probably do! Maybe you even have times when you're critical of yourself. Some of us get so impatient that we scold ourselves:

- "You forgot to pick up Dexter after soccer practice!"
- "You *knew* you wouldn't have time to make that wedding dress! . . . *Now what?*"
- "How could you just stand there and let her pull that gallon of milk out of the fridge?"
- "*Why* are you so slow?"
- "How could you have said that to Ralph?"
- "What were you *thinking?*"

Would we be so harsh if we went back and talked to ourselves when we were just a little baby?

- "Why can't you walk yet? Your brother Eddie walked when he was just nine months old, and you're a *year* old! What's wrong with you?"
- When you were two and a half or so: "How come you can't talk? Look at that little neighbor kid Adelaide—she can talk in complete sentences, and you can hardly say anything!"
- When you were learning to write: "Can't you tell the difference between an *I* and an *L*? *Think!*"
- When you were just starting piano lessons: "For goodness sakes . . . Can't you just *once* play something other than 'Loudly Brays the Donkey?'"
- Your first day at school: "*Buck up!*"
- Your first time away from home: "*Grow up!*"

These are likely *not* things you would say to yourself back then . . . but think of some of the things you say to yourself now! Do you ever get up in the morning, and before you're completely awake, you look in the mirror and are shocked at who's looking back at you?

"Who is that old woman? Are you my mother?"

"Why can't you be pretty like Sophia Loren?"

"Why are you so *slow*! You bug me!"

"You're not going to wear *that*, are you?"

What Are Some of the Causes of This Impatience?

Maybe part of our problem is that we live in a culture and society where we're so busy—perhaps too busy! And we're used to having things be "instant." We may feel that we have to be Wonder Woman in every single aspect of our lives—every single minute of every single day. We may wear ourselves out trying to be all things to all people, keeping up appearances.

Is It "Bad" to Be Impatient with Ourselves?

Well, I think it makes it difficult for us to be truly happy, to enjoy more of our days and experiences. Impatience can bring discouragement, stress, fear, doubt, a loss of hope—and even feelings of failure.

Is Patience a Positive Thing, Then?

Yes, it is. It's a virtue—a spiritual gift—a divine attribute! Developing patience can be painful, but the fruits are so sweet!

I've heard that "patience is when you've learned to hide your impatience." Or that it's the ability to idle your motor when you feel like stripping your gears!

Why Is Patience So Important?

Because anger is corrupting and degrading. A wise man said that a single moment of anger can destroy the results of many years of positive deeds. For every minute you're angry you lose sixty seconds of happiness. Anger is hard work, and patience is the antidote for anger. (Call the Poison Control Center—they'll tell you the same thing.)

Patience: A Gift of the Spirit, a Divine Attribute

Patience is a form of self-discipline, self-control, and respect. It requires faith and trust, and it isn't about just waiting, although sometimes it takes as much courage to *wait* as it does to *act*. Being patient with others (and yourself) is a way of showing respect.

Impatience Is a Form of Contention

It's a symptom of selfishness, and it's often a sign that we're trying to do too much. Remember this counsel: "Do not run faster or labor more than you have strength and means" (D&C 10:4).

Do You Ever Imagine Heavenly Father Being Impatient with You?

Do you think of Him looking down at you and saying something like, "You really annoy Me"? Someone here today may be thinking something along the lines of: *Every person in this room is better than I am, and Heavenly Father loves them more than He loves me.* That's not fair, is it? Not for One whose hand is stretched out still (see Isaiah 9:12, 17, 21). "Christ had patience. . . . He was never excited, in a hurry. He endured uncomplainingly. Knowing early as He must have known, that He was the Christ, He yet shows no impatience during thirty years to begin His mission. He patiently waited."[2] Our Heavenly Father and the Savior have perfect love and infinite patience for us:

- "Be patient in afflictions, for thou shalt have many; but endure them, for, lo, I am with thee, even unto the end of thy days" (D&C 24:8).
- "I will not leave you comfortless: I will come to you" (John 14:18).
- "Do not fear, for I the Lord am with you, and will stand by you" (D&C 68:6).
- "I will never leave thee, nor forsake thee" (Hebrews 13:5).
- "Be of good cheer, little children; for I am in your midst, and I have not forsaken you" (D&C 61:36).

You really *are* a child of God, and He really *does* love you! If you're not convinced that this is true, why don't you ask Him? And then listen for His response. *Are you really my Heavenly Father? Do you love me even with all my weaknesses? Is there hope for me to make it back home to you?*

Remember what President Dieter F. Uchtdorf said? "Stop it!"[3] (Okay, that wasn't exactly what I had written down . . .) He said: "You are closer to heaven than you suppose."[4] *You really are!*

How about a little "scripture chase?" Just raise your hand if you know where these verses are found.

- "I will go and do the things which the Lord hath commanded all at once."
- "Be ye therefore perfect by tomorrow afternoon."

I think it takes longer. "Wherefore, continue in patience until ye are perfected" (D&C 67:13).

Where does it say, "Love thy neighbor—but not thyself"?

I Get Impatient with Myself

For one thing, I'm CDO. (It's the same as OCD, but I put all the letters in alphabetical order.) Let me give you an example of obsessive behavior which I have *finally* let go: I used to have to go to "zero" when I filled my car. Sometimes I even spilled gas trying to get there. I may have been at $8.23, and I had go to $8.30. (That's when gas was a whole lot cheaper!) I remember spilling gas on my shoe once and thinking, *This is stupid! You are so stupid! Let it go!* And it took a while, but I don't even think about it anymore—except for this talk, so it's all your fault. ☺

Maybe you can look back and realize that you've been able to make some changes too—changes which are a lot more important than filling your car with gas. I've been working on patience my whole life—over seventy-two years! And I admit I've made some progress. (Let's hope!)

Happily (and fortunately), patience is a virtue that can be cultivated and nurtured over time. We can make a difference in our lives—we really can. We need to be patient with our efforts to develop patience. We tend to be our own worst critics, to judge ourselves so harshly. We *all* make mistakes; we *all* have things we need and want to change.

I'll share a few strategies which have been helpful to me:

I try to identify the things that most often influence me to lose my patience. What are the events, the people, the phrases, or the circumstances that always seem to cause you to lose your cool? Watch yourself, and figure it out.

Write things down. This might help more than you think it will. One way to relieve stress is to write about it. Write down what was happening when you lost your patience this morning (or yesterday, or whenever). What happened, and how did you respond? What (if anything) would you like to have done differently? Becoming more aware of when and how you lose your patience (and your temper) can help you to work on a different response.

Maybe you'll find that there are certain things which occur more frequently than others—pay attention to what they are, and see what you can do to avoid getting so mad at yourself (and others) so quickly.

Try to figure out why you're in such a hurry. Do you ever lose patience with yourself because you're multitasking, or you're on a too-tight schedule? If you're stretching yourself too thin, it may help to "chop-chop" your to-do list. Sometimes it feels so good to just be *list-less*! See if you can delegate some responsibilities to others. Slow down—don't sweat the small stuff.

Not everything *can* be "instant," even in a society where so many things are advertised that way. Most good things take time—they can't be rushed, and that includes relationships (with family, with friends and neighbors, and also with your Heavenly Father).

Find some healthy ways to relieve frustration. Punch a pillow. Juggle some oranges. Run around the block or up and down the stairs. Count to ten slowly—or to one hundred if you need to (and have time). Warn those near you to *run for their lives*! (To one of your children: "Honey, Mommy is going to shut her eyes and slowly count to ten. You go hide!") In some situations you might say to someone: "I can feel that I'm about to lose my cool . . . just give me a minute!" If you don't know what else to do in any situation, just be quiet.

I often use humor when I feel myself getting impatient. I talk to myself. I'll say things like:

Oh, you must be so proud of yourself right now!

I think this is a chance for a do-over.

Erase! Erase!

Slow down!

Or just a simple apology to myself:

I'm sorry—I'm doing the best I can right now.

Sometimes you just have to laugh at yourself. Life should be *enjoyable*. It should have lots of moments and experiences which are just plain fun. How many of you have taken a picture of a mess your child made instead of losing patience?

Many find that humor helps them hang on to patience in some very trying circumstances. Here's an example:

The exhausted clerk had pulled down blanket after blanket from the shelf, but still the female customer was not satisfied.

"There is one more blanket left," said the clerk. "Do you care to see it?"

"I'm not going to buy one today," said the woman. "I've only been looking for a friend."

"Well," said the clerk, "I'll take the last one down if you think your friend might be in it."

It's a Fact That It Takes Patience to Raise Children

I ran across a list of several simple tests to determine your readiness for children. I'll share just a few with you (you'll get the idea):

Mess Test

Smear peanut butter (with or without nuts) on the sofa and curtains. Now rub your hands in the cat's litter box, then on the walls. Cover the stains with a coating of crayon (pick a color . . . any color). Place a fish-stick behind the couch and leave it there all summer.

Toy Test

Obtain a fifty-five-gallon container of Legos (or you can substitute roofing tacks or broken bottles). Have a friend spread them all over the house. Put on a blindfold. Now try to walk to the bathroom or the kitchen barefoot. Do not shout naughty words, as this could wake a sleeping child.

Feeding Test

Obtain a large plastic jug. Fill it halfway with milk. Suspend the jug from the ceiling and start the jug swinging. Try to insert spoons full of applesauce into the mouth of the jug while pretending to be an airplane. Once you've succeeded, dump the contents of the jug on the floor.

Grocery Store Test

Borrow one or two small animals (goats are best) and take them with you to the grocery store. Keep them in sight and pay for anything they eat or damage.

It does take patience to raise children!

STOP HOLDING YOURSELF (AND OTHERS) TO UNREACHABLE STANDARDS

Sure, we'd all be more patient if babies didn't cry, dishes didn't break, computers didn't crash, traffic didn't back up, nothing ever spilled, lines were never long, and people *never* made mistakes . . . but we're not living in the millennium yet. And nobody's perfect . . . yet—I know some of you are pretty close.

Impatience is often the result of unfulfilled expectations. See if you can get rid of some of your many musts and shoulds. Can't keep up with the dust? Well, dust protects furniture!

TAKE A BREAK! TAKE A TIME OUT!

Step away from the problem (the impatience), even for just a few seconds. Take time, as you can, to do absolutely nothing. Just sit quietly and think. Don't watch TV, don't read, don't look through a magazine or catalogue . . . just "chill."

Do you ever just go somewhere without your cell phone? (I hear gasping! I'm hearing some gasping!) Elder Richard G. Scott invited us to "remove [our] watch[es] when [we] enter a house of the Lord."[5] Doing that has made a difference for me.

Learn to say: "I don't know." There's nothing wrong with that. And learn to say no to requests you can't reasonably respond to. There's nothing wrong with that, either. How would you like to have some excuses to use when you can't think of your own?

They won't know what to say! "Oh! Well! . . . I see . . . hmmmm . . ."

(And then they thank you! And they hang up!)

Here you go (and when you try one or more of these, I'd love to hear what happened):

You'll usually begin with "I'm sorry, but I won't be able to," then:

" . . . I'm sculpting a frog out of cottage cheese."

" . . . I'm memorizing my social security number."

" . . . I'm an understudy for a matador. His name's Al . . . he got gored!"

" . . . My mother-in-law said she might drop by."

" . . . I'm working on a poem about mosquitoes, and I need to focus."

" . . . I've lost my marbles, and I'm worthless without them."

" . . . I'm in a race with Motel 6 to see who can do the most laundry!"

And the one I use most:

" . . . I would if I could, but I can't."

Practice Being Patient

Becoming more patient doesn't happen overnight. You have to *want* it, and it takes a lot of practice . . . And yes, it takes some failures as well as some successes. But oh, if you've been working on it, doesn't it feel *good* when you can tell you've made some progress? Let Heavenly Father know, as you communicate with Him openly and often, that you need heavenly help to be patient with yourself. Do all you can to be sensitive to the promptings of the Holy Ghost.

Start Small

You can't become as patient as you want to be in twenty minutes, right? Start with something small and manageable. What are some of the things which make you just a little bit mad? Start there. Focus on those and try to have the bigger things wait for a while.

Ponder and Meditate

This doesn't even mean you have to plan for an hour a day or something (but wouldn't that be wonderful!). A lot of things can get sorted out as you pray and ponder.

Remember What Matters Most to You

Decide and remember what your highest priorities are. What are they? Are you able to keep first things first?

WHEN THERE ARE THINGS YOU CAN'T CHANGE, CAN'T RESOLVE, SOMETIMES YOU JUST HAVE TO LET GO

Life is unpredictable and there are many circumstances that are outside of our control. Expect the unexpected. This is all much easier said than done. Especially if you're hoping to change someone else. (Is there anyone on your list? A child? A spouse? A coworker? A friend?) Maybe *you're* on someone's list! I'm just saying that changing ourselves is possible, and whether or not others change is up to them. Keep being a good example.

We often speak of "the patience of Job." While his patience is extraordinary, I believe that even the most impatient of us can learn to be more patient. So be kind to yourself. Be gentle. Have you noticed that you're sometimes kinder to others—even people you don't know—than you are to *yourself*? Sometimes our impatience with ourselves keeps us from being as kind and loving with others as we want to be.

Patience is a virtue, and by linking it to faith, we take another step toward becoming more like the Savior. Elder Neal A. Maxwell said, "Patience is not only one of the virtues resulting from being a true believer in Christ, it is also . . . essential . . . in the process of bringing about all the other virtues."[6]

So, dear friends, if you feel that impatience with yourself is a weakness, remember that with God's help you can turn this into a strength. Do what you can to protect the power of patience in your life.

Is there anyone in your life who needs to hear you say "I love you"? Not just "Love ya!" but "I love you"? Is there anyone who needs an apology from you? Anyone who needs your forgiveness? Do you need to be less judgmental of yourself? Some of these personal journeys are long and painful. You know that, and I know that. Don't give up. Don't ever label yourself a failure. Try not to give in to the feeling that you just can't do it.

Elder Maxwell also said, "When in situations of stress we wonder if there is any more in us to give, we can be comforted to know that God, who knows our capacity perfectly, placed us here to succeed. No one was foreordained to fail or to be wicked (D&C 50:40)."[7]

Listen to phrases from a few of our hymns:

"As thy days may demand, so thy succor shall be."[8]

"Guide me as I search in weakness; / Let thy loving light be mine."[9]

"He answers privately, / Reaches my reaching."[10]

"Earth has no sorrow that heav'n cannot heal."[11]

When you feel you're getting impatient with yourself, close your eyes and remember that you are closer to many who love you dearly than you can imagine.

Maybe it's your mother or your father, and maybe they're both gone, but we've been taught that those who have gone before us are very, very close. They don't just "check on you" once in a while. Feel them giving you encouragement, comfort, ideas, and perfect love. Elder Orson F. Whitney wrote: "No pain that we suffer, no trial that we experience is wasted. It ministers to our education, to the development of such qualities as patience, faith, fortitude and humility. All that we suffer and all that we endure, *especially when we endure it patiently*, builds up our characters, purifies our hearts, expands our souls, and makes us more tender and charitable, more worthy to be called the children of God. . . . and it is through sorrow and suffering, toil and tribulation, that we gain the education that we came here to acquire and which will make us more like our Father and Mother in heaven."[12] Think of them, your Heavenly Parents. I think we can't even imagine the depth of their love for us—both of them!

"In the heav'ns are parents single? / No, the thought makes reason stare! / Truth is reason; truth eternal / Tells me I've a *mother* there."[13]

"God is our refuge and strength, a very present help in trouble" (Psalm 46:1).

"Come boldly unto the throne of grace, that [you] may obtain mercy, and find grace to help in time of need" (Hebrews 4:16).

Jesus calmed the seas, and He can calm *you*. When you feel discouraged, He cares. When you feel abandoned and alone, He is there. When you feel worthless or hopeless, He'll lift you. When you feel lost, He'll light your way. When you weep, He weeps with you. When you are impatient, He is infinitely patient with you. When you don't know where to turn, He opens his arms and says, "Come unto me" (Matthew 11:28). "His love will find you and gently lead you / From darkest night into day."[14] Come unto Him—come unto Jesus.

NOTES

1. Dieter F. Uchtdorf, "Forget Me Not," *Ensign*, November 2011, 123.
2. John Henry Evans, "The New Testament in Literature and History," *Improvement Era*, vol. 15, no. 12 (October 1912): 1055–56.
3. Uchtdorf, "The Merciful Obtain Mercy," *Ensign*, May 2012, 75.
4. Uchtdorf, "Forget Me Not," 123.
5. Richard G. Scott, "Temple Worship: The Source of Strength and Power in Times of Need," *Ensign*, May 2009, 43.
6. Neal A. Maxwell, *Notwithstanding My Weakness* (Salt Lake City: Deseret Book, 1981), 59.
7. Maxwell, "Meeting the Challenges of Today," Brigham Young University devotional, 10 October 1978; available at http://speeches.byu.edu/?act=viewitem&id=909; accessed 17 October 2012.
8. Attributed to Robert Keen, "How Firm a Foundation," *Hymns of The Church of Jesus Christ of Latter-day Saints* (Salt Lake City: The Church of Jesus Christ of Latter-day Saints, 1985), no. 85.
9. John A. Widtsoe, "Lead Me into Life Eternal," *Hymns*, no. 45.
10. Emma Lou Thayne, "Where Can I Turn for Peace?" *Hymns*, no. 129.
11. Thomas Moore, "Come, Ye Disconsolate," *Hymns*, no. 115.
12. Orson F. Whitney, cited by Spencer W. Kimball in *Faith Precedes the Miracle* (Salt Lake City: Deseret Book, 1972), 98; emphasis added.
13. Eliza R. Snow, "O My Father," *Hymns*, no. 292; emphasis added.
14. Orson Pratt Huish, "Come unto Jesus," *Hymns*, no. 117.

Live Like His Son

Ann M. Dibb

Powerful eternal truths are contained in the doctrine of the plan of salvation and its associated mortal path. In the scriptures, the plan is referred to as "'the plan of salvation' (Alma 24:14; Moses 6:62), 'the great plan of happiness' (Alma 42:8), 'the plan of redemption' (Jacob 6:8; Alma 12:30), and 'the plan of mercy' (Alma 42:15)."[1]

We know that we are the spiritual sons and daughters of God. Before we gained our physical bodies, we were involved in a council with all of Heavenly Father's children. While participating in this council, we were taught and we accepted our Father's plan.

Even though we would become mortal, experience the weaknesses associated with a physical body, and have to withstand the temptations of the adversary, we were confident in our ability to remain faithful. We listened as our Savior, Jesus Christ, expressed His willingness to come to earth. He volunteered to come and show us the way; He would provide "the truth, and the life" (John 14:6). We would come to know the Father by looking to His Son, for They are one in purpose. He alone would have the power to lay down His life and take it up again, because He would

---

Ann M. Dibb is the second counselor in the Young Women general presidency. She is the daughter of President Thomas S. Monson and Sister Frances J. Monson. Ann was born and raised in Salt Lake City and earned her bachelor's degree at Brigham Young University in elementary education. She has served in each of the Church auxiliaries, including as a member of the Young Women general board. She and her husband, Roger Dibb, are the parents of one daughter and three sons.

be the Son of God and the Son of Man. Jesus Christ covenanted to be our Savior and Redeemer (see Moses 4:2; Abraham 3:27). God's prophets have revealed that we shouted for joy when we learned of Jesus Christ's willing sacrifice in our behalf (see Job 38:7). And Jesus humbly declared that through it all, the glory would be the Father's.

Satan rejected the Father's plan and rebelled. He sought to disallow the law of agency and to claim all the glory. Fortunately, we chose to follow Heavenly Father's plan.

We were forewarned: life's mortal journey, or path, would be challenging. We would make mistakes. But through Christ's selfless sacrifice, when we committed sin, we could repent, change, seek forgiveness, and become clean again. We would exercise our agency in choosing righteousness, choosing to follow Jesus Christ, and rejecting Satan.

We are now experiencing mortality. Our spirit is united with a mortal, physical body. We are faced with opportunities to exercise our agency daily, and we strive to follow Jesus Christ by making correct choices.

Sister Rosemary Wixom spoke at BYU's Women's Conference as the newly called general Primary president. I loved her message. She taught about the plan and our journey on this mortal path. She encouraged us to *stay on the path* and help others remain on the path back to our Heavenly Father. She then demonstrated this truth by having us make the American Sign Language action for the phrase, "I will stay on the path back to my Heavenly Father."[2] When I copied her actions, I felt the Spirit confirm to me the promise I made in premortal realms, "Yes, I will stay on the path back to my Heavenly Father."

All of us made this promise. Now the question is: how will we fulfill it? The answer is that we will exercise faith in our Savior Jesus Christ and the plan. We will accept His gospel and keep His commandments. When we sin, we will repent. We will accept and honor sacred ordinances and covenants; first, the ordinance and covenant of baptism and of the gift of the Holy Ghost, and second, sacred temple ordinances and covenants. We will choose to accept the Holy Ghost and keep ourselves worthy of His constant companionship. We will endure and serve until we complete our mortal probation. We understand that opposition is necessary to develop spiritual strength, and we are willing to withstand this as we choose to follow our Savior, Jesus Christ. We look forward to the day when we will humbly return to the presence of the Father and His Son and receive our promised reward, exaltation.

I have just shared with you the Sunday School and Young Women version of the plan of salvation. I believe it. I love it. I teach it. And I strive to live in such a way so as to achieve its ultimate promises. There's just one problem—*it is a lot harder than it sounds.*

My friend, *my* Young Women leader, has experienced multiple challenges in her seventy years of mortality. She is remarkable. Long ago she said to me, "Ann, I know I heard all that would be expected of me, and I willingly accepted what would be required as explained in that premortal council. But sometimes I wonder if instead of listening to the plan and what would be expected of me, I was talking!"

I know we may at times *think* this, but it is not true. We knew, we accepted, and we were confident in our ability to succeed. We rejoiced. We came to this earth so that we might gain experience. *Hearing* about an experience and *actually having it* are two very different things! I believe that in our *innocence* we *thought* we understood all that our mortal journey would require of us. We did not. We could not fully understand until we'd actually *experienced* it for ourselves.

I came to a new understanding of the importance of gaining experience as I read Mark Twain's essay, "Eve Speaks," an early version of what became his *Diaries of Adam and Eve.* In this mostly humorous essay, feelings and experiences that may have taken place are recounted. I was moved by what Eve may have felt after leaving the Garden. Eve shares: "We were ignorant then; we are rich in learning now—ah, how rich! We know hunger, thirst and cold; we know pain, disease, and grief; we know hate, rebellion, and deceit; we know remorse, . . . we know weariness of body and spirit, the unrefreshing sleep, the rest which rests not, the dreams which restore Eden, and banish it again with the waking; . . . we know right from wrong, . . . we know all the rich product of the Moral Sense, and it is our possession. Would we could sell it for one hour of Eden and white purity. . . . We have it all—that treasure."[3]

In Moses 5:10–12, we read our first parents' learnings. Adam declares, "Blessed be the name of God, for because of my transgression my eyes are opened, and in this life I shall have joy, and again in the flesh I shall see God. And Eve, his wife, heard all these things and was glad, saying: Were it not for our transgression we never should have had seed, and never should have known good and evil, and the joy of our redemption, and the eternal life which God giveth unto all the obedient. And Adam and Eve blessed the name of God, and they made all things known unto their sons and their daughters."

When we think of the path, we may think of a straight, level road. Or we may think of a road that forks into two, forcing us to choose between them. We're all familiar with Robert Frost's poetic lines: "Two roads diverged in a wood, and I— / I took the one less traveled by, / and that has made all the difference."[4]

The idea that Mr. Frost beautifully brings to life in this poem, of choosing your own path, is an important one. We are all trying to stay on the path that leads back to our Heavenly Father. But sometimes, by my own choice, I may wander from the path and find my road unpleasant, unsightly, or even closed. Sometimes I find myself on a bumpy, challenging road I *didn't* consciously choose. Whether by our own choices or circumstances out of our control, the journey is at times difficult and threatens mortal and eternal consequences. Some paths are frightening and dangerous, with serious inclines. There are chains mounted in the rocks nearby in order to give me something to hold on to during my ascent. Some of us may fall while traveling the path. Is all of this effort and challenge necessary? Yes, it is, because this is the way we are refined and strengthened. This is how we become fit and prepared for the next mountain, which we will soon have the opportunity to climb and enjoy incredible vistas from its peak. This is the way we become the people God knows we can become.

For some, the path may be like that dreaded childhood game "Chutes and Ladders." We travel so far and get so close—only to tumble downward as though falling into an abyss. However, it is when we are in the abyss, looking upward to the light of Christ through the darkness, that we begin to hear the voice of the Lord and heed the promptings of the Holy Ghost. All pride is suddenly stripped away, and we begin to acquire the Christlike attribute of humility. Now we are willing to submit our will and accept His ever-outstretched hand. In hardship, our hearts are softened and changed, and we begin to see with spiritual eyes the end we earnestly seek and how to get there.

Consider our individual lives, the road each of us is traveling. No two roads look exactly alike. Look around at the women assembled in this hall. Standing up here, I think you look perfect. You could be on the cover of the *Ensign* or the *Liahona*! Just looking at you, it seems *your* path is perfect. *You probably know differently*. For a moment, let's participate in a brief little activity. Please lower your head and close your eyes. I'm going to name a few concerns that may affect you. When I say something that applies to you, will you raise your hand? Keep your hand upheld until I tell you to lower it. Remember, eyes closed.

Let's begin. Raise your hand if your family has been affected by financial troubles. By loss of employment. Raise your hand if you haven't had the opportunity to be sealed to a righteous companion. Have you experienced health challenges, either physical or emotional? Infertility? The effects of aging? Raise your hand if your family has been affected by anything that is not considered virtuous, lovely, of good report, or praiseworthy. Has your family been affected by someone's unrighteous use of agency or selfishness? Dishonesty? Even simple poor judgment? Have you had problems with your children, spouse, parents, or siblings? Raise your hand if someone in your family has experienced loss of personal testimony. Gender challenges? The death of a loved one? Do you ever feel lonely or overwhelmed? Have you needed to repent or practice forgiveness? Raise your hand if you feel you have not received blessings you feel you have earned through your personal righteousness. Raise your hand if your amazing eighteen-year-old child did not get accepted to Brigham Young University. And finally, raise your hand if you feel, at times, as though your heart has been broken.

Sisters, keep your hands up, but raise your head and open your eyes. Look around and observe those assembled in this hall. You may now lower your hands.

It would probably be easier for me to ask, "Raise your hand if your life is perfect, turning out just as you'd hoped for and planned." Now, if by some minute chance you were getting ready to raise your hand, don't—this could clearly be injurious to your health and safety!

I want to thank the sisters for singing one of my favorite Primary songs, "He Sent His Son." Frequently when I have a question or have struggles, I'll stop and think, *What am I to do? How will I solve this problem? How will I endure what I'm called upon to endure, travel this path I'm expected to traverse and do so successfully?* For me, the answer lies within the words of this song: "Have faith, have hope, live like his Son, help others on their way. . . . Live like his Son."[5]

When I doubt my abilities to follow those words, I find myself asking another question: *Is there no other way?* I love the counsel Alma gives to his son Shiblon: "And now, my son, I have told you this that ye may learn wisdom, that ye may learn of me that there is no other way or means whereby man can be saved, only in and through Christ. Behold, he is the life and the light of the world. Behold, he is the word of truth and righteousness" (Alma 38:9). And so, because there is no other way to return to our Heavenly Father than in and through Christ, we must submit our personal will, be obedient, and press forward. The words from the song that encourage me so well can serve as guideposts along our way, no matter how difficult the path.

FIRST, "HAVE FAITH"

We know faith is a principle that requires action, effort, and obedience. Elder L. Whitney Clayton teaches: "Faith . . . is a spiritual gift. Faith increases when we not only hear, but act on the word of God as well, in obedience to the truths we have been taught."[6] Nephi taught that all must come to accept Jesus Christ as their Savior. "He manifesteth himself unto all those who believe in him, by the power of the Holy Ghost; yea, unto every nation, kindred, tongue, and people, working mighty miracles, signs, and wonders, among the children of men according to their faith" (2 Nephi 26:13).

However, at times we may identify more with the humbling story of the man who sought Christ's healing power for his son and possibly himself. We read in Mark the account of the father who pleaded, "But if thou canst do any thing, have compassion on us, and help us. Jesus said unto him, If thou canst believe, all things are possible to him that believeth. And straightway the father of the child cried out, and said with tears, Lord, I believe; help thou mine unbelief" (Mark 9:22–24). And the Savior healed the son. Have faith.

Second, "Have Hope"

Hope, too, is a spiritual gift. We have hope when we trust in God's promises.[7] Hope is based on our *experience*. One way our hope is strengthened is by choosing to act on the teachings of prophets, ancient and modern day. Moroni taught, "Whoso believeth in God might with surety hope for a better world, yea, even a place at the right hand of God, which hope cometh of faith, maketh an anchor to the souls of men, which would make them sure and steadfast, always abounding in good works, being led to glorify God" (Ether 12:4). Paul taught: "We glory in tribulations also: knowing that tribulation worketh patience; and patience, experience; and experience, hope: and hope maketh not ashamed; because the love of God is shed abroad in our hearts by the Holy Ghost which is given unto us" (Romans 5:3–5).

President Dieter F. Uchtdorf frequently bears testimony concerning the necessity of having hope. He has said, "Hope is not knowledge, but rather the abiding trust that the Lord will fulfill His promise to us."[8] It was revealed to Joseph Smith while in Liberty Jail, "My son, peace be unto thy soul; thine adversity and thine afflictions shall be but a small moment" (D&C 121:7). Have hope.

Third, "Live Like His Son"

The surest guide to help us on our mortal path is our Savior's perfect example. Jesus Christ glorified his Father through His constant obedience. I love the simple but powerful counsel the Savior provided to His disciples and to us: "If ye love me, keep my commandments" (John 14:15). The Savior loved His Father, and He kept His Father's commandments. The Savior loves us. He was honest in keeping His covenants with Heavenly Father and with us by fulfilling the infinite Atonement. He kept the commandments, and so must we.

The recently revised *For the Strength of Youth* contains the Ten Commandments as well as the two "great commandments."[9] Both provide the foundation of moral law. They are eternal gospel principles that are necessary for our peace and happiness now and for eternity.[10]

Jesus taught the Ten Commandments in His Sermon on the Mount. He summarized them when He responded to the pointed question offered by the young lawyer, who said, tempting him, "Master, which is the great commandment in the law? Jesus said unto him, Thou shalt love the Lord thy God with all thy heart, and with all thy soul, and with all thy mind. This is the first and great commandment. And the second is like unto it, Thou shalt love thy neighbour as thyself. On these two commandments hang all the law and the prophets" (Matthew 22:36–40).

All prophets teach of the importance of obeying God's commandments. President Thomas S. Monson is no exception. In his address "May You Have Courage," he quoted the television newsman Ted Koppel: "What Moses brought down from Mt. Sinai were not the Ten Suggestions, they are Commandments. *Are*, not were."[11] Keeping the commandments is a sure way to stay firmly anchored on the right path.

LAST, "HELP OTHERS ON THEIR WAY"

It is our responsibility and privilege to help others who share or cross our path. We are called upon to "strengthen [our] brethren" (Luke 22:32) and "lift up the hands which hang down, and strengthen the feeble knees" (D&C 81:5). We do not always choose who accompanies us on our path or the lessons we must learn through our shared experience. Many times we walk with people who stretch our capacity, understanding, abilities, and patience. In times like these, we truly must seek the Savior's enabling power.

Conversely, there are times when we cross paths with individuals who seem to be answers to our prayers, literally the angels promised to bear us up (see D&C 84:88). It is a blessing to experience each of these moments.

On our journeys, we may hunger for a simple expression of acknowledgement and encouragement. May I suggest, never forget the power of sending a note to someone expressing your sincere, specific thoughts and love. I have heard Elder Jeffrey R. Holland relate, "Remember, in order to receive a note, you have to send a note. It's just the way it works." While preparing this talk, I reread some of the notes I have received. My tears flowed, and my feelings of love increased—love not only for the friend who wrote the note but also for my Heavenly Father. It was as though in receiving and rereading the note, I was reminded that He is ever watchful over me. He watched over me by prompting a friend to write a note.

Statements, mantras, or family expressions can also buoy us up. When I am challenged, I sometimes think of the statement from the movie spoof *Galaxy Quest*: "Never give up. Never surrender."[12] Recently, I learned that a woman in Florida bore her testimony of the comfort she received when she heard President Monson's simple words of encouragement in a general Young Women meeting. She said, "'Life by the yard is hard. By the inch, it's a cinch.'[13] I've been saying this statement aloud multiple times each day, and it seems as though my burdens have become lighter!" Once when I was traveling with my father to The Gila Valley Arizona Temple dedication, a woman shared her grandmother's favorite expression: "Just focus on the gospel. This, too, shall pass." These statements contain reassuring words that help us on our way.

When we help others, we exhibit charity, the pure love of Christ, which we know "never faileth" (Moroni 7:46). An upbeat hymn reminds me to have charity, and it immediately makes me think of my father: "Scatter sunshine all along your way. / Cheer and bless and brighten ev'ry passing day."[14] President Monson has taught, "There is a serious need for the charity that gives attention to those who are unnoticed, hope to those who are discouraged, aid to those who are afflicted. True charity is love in action. The need for charity is everywhere."[15]

I can testify that President Monson doesn't simply teach of charity; he lives it. I'll share two simple interactions. My husband Roger is a CPA and had just completed yet another tax season. One of his clients, a seventy-four-year-old widow, shared, "You know, I'm not a member of your church, but I met your father-in-law. I saw him in the hallway at a Jazz game, and he greeted me with a cheery 'Hello' and shook my hand. My daughter joined your church, and she can't believe *my* luck in meeting the prophet." The woman then said about President Monson: "He's a friendly fellow, isn't he?" Yes, he is.

About a month ago, I accompanied my father to church in his home ward, the ward where I grew up. After a wonderful sacrament meeting, my father was walking to his car. Two little boys, maybe four years old, came outside. You could tell they were glad to be out of church. Their shirts were unbuttoned and their ties hung loose and crooked. No parents were present. There were no cameras. One boy cautiously approached President Monson and asked, "Can you wiggo yo ears?" My father looked a bit confused; I could sense he didn't understand what the little boy had said. I translated for him and waited. My father said nothing, so I looked over and saw that dad was wiggling his ears. The little boy smiled broadly, turned to his friend, and said, "See, he can wiggo his ears." Happily they ran away. It was such a sweet little moment. President Monson happily helps people on their way, whether they're seventy-four or four, and we can too.

God the Father's eternal plan of salvation is real. We are all living it as we travel our individual mortal path: learning, choosing, praying, serving, loving, repenting, forgiving, experiencing sorrow and pain, and experiencing joy. It may be difficult at times, but we will not let temporary discouragement overcome us. We must do as the grandmother in Arizona counseled: "Just focus on the gospel. This, too, shall pass."

Let us each choose to believe and follow our Savior. He teaches us to be of good cheer. He shows us the way; He is the truth and the life. May we continually move forward on our path, having faith and hope, living "like His Son," and helping others on their way as we journey to our promised eternal joy, our peace and exaltation, is my humble prayer.

Notes

1. *True to the Faith* (Salt Lake City: The Church of Jesus Christ of Latter-day Saints, 2004), 115.
2. Rosemary Wixom, "The Plan of Salvation: One of Heaven's Best Gifts to Mankind," BYU Women's Conference, 29 April 2011, 9; available at http://ce.byu.edu/cw/womensconference/archive/2011/pdf/Rosemary_W._Wixom.pdf; accessed 8 October 2012.
3. Mark Twain, "Eve Speaks," in *The Complete Essays of Mark Twain* (Boston: Da Capo Press, 1991), 622–23.
4. Robert Frost, "The Road Not Taken," in *Mountain Interval* (New York: Henry Holt, 1916), 9.
5. Mabel Jones Gabbott, "He Sent His Son," *Children's Songbook* (Salt Lake City: The Church of Jesus Christ of Latter-day Saints, 1989), 34–35.
6. L. Whitney Clayton, "'Help Thou Mine Unbelief,'" *Ensign*, November 2001, 28.

7. See *True to the Faith* (Salt Lake City: The Church of Jesus Christ of Latter-day Saints, 2004), 85–86.
8. Dieter F. Uchtdorf, "The Infinite Power of Hope," *Ensign*, November 2008, 22.
9. See *For the Strength of Youth* (Salt Lake City: The Church of Jesus Christ of Latter-day Saints, 2011), 44.
10. See "Obedience," *True to the Faith*, 108–9.
11. Ted Koppel, Duke University commencement address, 1987; in Thomas S. Monson, "May You Have Courage," *Ensign*, May 2009, 125; emphasis added.
12. See *Galaxy Quest*, imdb.com; available at http://www.imdb.com/title/tt0177789/quotes; accessed 8 October 2012.
13. Monson, "Believe, Obey, and Endure," *Ensign*, May 2012, 129.
14. Lanta Wilson Smith, "Scatter Sunshine," *Hymns of The Church of Jesus Christ of Latter-day Saints* (Salt Lake City: The Church of Jesus Christ of Latter-day Saints, 1985), no. 230.
15. Monson, "Charity Never Faileth," *Ensign*, November 2010, 124.

The Path of Knowledge, Service, and Traditions

Sarah Steele

"My life is a gift; my life has a plan. / My life has a purpose; in heaven it began. / My choice was to come to this lovely home on earth / And seek for God's light to direct me from birth."[1]

Before we came to this earth, we lived with our Heavenly Father. We loved Him and we wanted to become like Him. We knew that to do that, we must come to earth, receive a body, be tempted and tried, and ultimately prove faithful so that we could return to Him. Heavenly Father explained to us that the only way back would be to overcome physical death and also to overcome the effects of sin, which would come from making mistakes. But He would not expect that we accomplish this by ourselves. He provided a Savior for us, our loving Elder Brother, who would break the bands of death and provide a way for us to be washed clean from our sins. There were many who did not like this plan. We, however, were among the brave and the true. We accepted our Savior's plan. We knew that the journey would be hard, and the path would be long and arduous. But we were up for the task—we were faithful, and we were excited!

When I was younger, I envisioned my earthly path to look something like this: A long, smooth white painted boardwalk that led to a tropical oasis. I would skip along this path, never making a mistake, never

Sarah D. Steele is the daughter of Roger and Ann M. Dibb. She is a teacher, an artist, and musician. She and her husband, Jim, are the parents of three children.

experiencing any trials, and end up lounging under a palm tree sipping lemonade for the remainder of my days.

Photo courtesy Shutterstock.

As I have gotten a little bit older, and a little bit wiser—I have discovered that this idealistic pathway was not realistic. My earthly path looks more like this: A long uphill trail with twists and turns, bumps and rocks. It is still a beautiful path, winding through lush green meadows and, at times, overlooking breathtaking vistas. But it's not always easy. I need to work hard and seek for God's light to direct me along the way. What's more, I am not alone on this journey. It is my responsibility to help my family along the path.

Photo courtesy Shutterstock.

As I have pondered this earthly journey, my thoughts have turned to another difficult journey recorded in the Book of Mormon. After Lehi was commanded to flee into the wilderness, he and Sariah obediently gathered their children and began their journey on an unknown path. How difficult it must have been for Sariah to leave her friends, her belongings, and her comfortable home. It must have taken great faith to take that first step onto the unknown wilderness pathway. But the Lord did not leave Sariah and her family alone on their journey. In 1 Nephi 17:13, we read, "I will also be your light in the wilderness: and I will prepare the way before you, if it so be that ye shall keep my commandments; wherefore, inasmuch as ye shall keep my commandments ye shall be led towards the promised land; and ye shall know that it is by me that ye are led."

Just as the Lord provided His light for Lehi and Sariah's journey, He has promised to light our pathways as we journey through this mortal life. Isaiah 60:19 says, "The Lord shall be thine everlasting light." As we travel with our loved ones along life's pathway, it is our responsibility to seek for this light. We must keep His commandments, we must learn, and we must teach. The Lord does not merely flip on a light switch to brighten our way. He expects us to do our part.

President Dieter F. Uchtdorf said: "The gospel of Jesus Christ is not an obligation; it is a pathway. . . . The gospel is a light that penetrates mortality and illuminates the way before us."[2] The gospel of Jesus Christ will brighten our path and help us navigate the bumps and turns along the journey. I would like to discuss three gospel truths that have helped to keep my pathway bright, truths that will help lead us and our families to the promised land of eternal life.

First is the light of *knowledge*.

The importance of knowledge is a recurring theme both in scripture and in the teachings of latter-day prophets. We have repeatedly been counseled to obtain all of the spiritual and secular education we can in order to contribute wherever we may serve, whether it be in our homes, our wards, our workplaces, or our communities. President Henry B. Eyring said, "The Lord and His Church have always encouraged education to increase our ability to serve Him and our Heavenly Father's children. For each of us, whatever our talents, He has service for us to give. And to do it well always involves learning."[3] He continues by saying we must first seek spiritual knowledge and then seek secular knowledge.

"I will follow God's plan for me, / Holding fast to his word."[4]

His word is found as we diligently search the scriptures. The scriptures teach that each of us is a daughter of Heavenly Father and that we lived with Him before we were born. He wants us to return with our families to live with Him and His Son, Jesus Christ. As we seek to gain a greater knowledge of the scriptures, our path will be illuminated.

Early in the Restoration, the Lord gave the revelation found in Doctrine and Covenants 25 to Emma Smith. This revelation depicts the characteristics he desires in his daughters as they travel on the pathway of mortal life. One of those characteristics is seeking knowledge. The Lord told Emma, "And thou shalt be ordained under his hand to expound scriptures. . . . And thy time shall be given to writing, and to learning much" (D&C 25:7–8). I am sure that the knowledge Emma gained through her study of spiritual matters was passed down to her children. As mothers, grandmothers, sisters, and teachers, we have a great responsibility to share our knowledge with young children. This knowledge will help illuminate their pathways. President Spencer W. Kimball said, "We want our homes to be blessed with sister scriptorians. . . . After all, who has any greater need to 'treasure up' the truths of the gospel than do women and mothers who do so much nurturing and teaching?"[5]

One way in which our family seeks spiritual knowledge is by reciting and memorizing scriptures. Each night at dinner, we bless the food and then after the prayer, we recite a scripture. The scripture remains the same for an entire month. By the end of the month, everyone in the family has memorized the scripture. The children are usually the first to master their memorization, and they thoroughly enjoy catching Mom or Dad making a mistake. This teaching technique has also provided many dinner conversations about what the scriptures mean and how we can implement them in our lives.

It has been rewarding as a parent to see my children increase in their gospel knowledge. Several years ago, a new family moved in across the street. One afternoon, I was visiting with the mother as our children were playing in the yard. She asked which church I attended, and I responded, "The Church of Jesus Christ of Latter-Day Saints." She was curious, and asked "What does your church believe?" My oldest daughter, who was about eight at the time, was standing nearby. She had heard the question and quickly responded, "We believe in God the Eternal Father, and in His Son, Jesus Christ, and in the Holy Ghost . . . and in Santa Claus." Although her knowledge wasn't perfect, Emi had used one of her memorized scriptures to share the gospel of Jesus Christ. How grateful I was to see that light shining brightly on her pathway.

Learning much includes not only scriptures, but it may be broadened to include all truth. The Lord has instructed us to seek after anything virtuous, lovely, or of good report or praiseworthy. Because "the glory of God is intelligence" (D&C 93:36), the prophets have encouraged us to "learn much" in order to serve God and our families. In D&C 90:15, we learn that we are to be familiar with good books, languages, and cultures. When my siblings and I were young, my mom would read aloud to us. At night we would lay in our beds with our bedroom doors open. My mom would sit in the hallway and read aloud. She would also read aloud in the car on family trips. I knew that my mom had a love of good books, and I'm sure she in part gained that love of books from her father, President Thomas S. Monson. My grandfather always has a book in his briefcase. It may be a church publication, a biography, or a book on world events. He loves to read and increase his knowledge.

I have taken the examples of my mother and grandfather and have tried to expose my young family to good books. Daily reading time is an important part of our family routine, and my children love when I read aloud in the hallway at night or on long car trips. President Gordon B. Hinckley said, "Cultivate within [your children] a taste for the best. While they are very young, read to them the great stories which have become immortal because of the virtues they teach. Expose them to good books."[6] I know that as we seek both spiritual knowledge and also uplifting secular knowledge, we are enlightening our earthly pathways.

The second light is that of *service.*

The Lord has taught that "when [we] are in the service of our fellow beings [we] are only in the service of [our] God" (Mosiah 2:17). Service is probably one of the greatest ways we can make our pathway bright. When the path seems especially steep and difficult, service can "turn the night to day."[7] When we serve others, we lose ourselves, we realize our many blessings, and we draw nearer to our Heavenly Father. President Lorenzo Snow said, "When you find yourselves a little gloomy, look around you and find somebody that is in a worse plight than yourself; go to him and find out what the trouble is, then try to remove it with the wisdom which the Lord bestows upon you; and the first thing you know, your gloom is gone, you feel light, the Spirit of the Lord is upon you, and everything seems illuminated."[8] Our Savior, Jesus Christ, is the greatest example of giving service. His life was a mission to preach the gospel and serve His fellow men. In John 13:14–15, it says, "If I then, your Lord and Master, have washed your feet; ye also ought to wash one another's feet. For I have given you an example, that ye should do as I have done to you."

Look around—is there someone in your circle of acquaintances that you can serve? President Thomas S. Monson has said, "The needs of others are ever present, and each of us can do something to help someone."[9] That someone might be an individual from your own family, it might be a neighbor, or it might be a member of your ward. When I think of service, I think of my mother-in-law, who tirelessly served her aging parents in their final years. While struggling with health challenges of her own, she saw to the physical, spiritual, and mental care of a mother with Alzheimer's disease and a father who had suffered from a serious stroke. Her children worried about her ability to keep up with this rigorous and challenging service. But Charlene never complained; rather, she flourished. She testified that through the power of prayer and scripture study she was sustained in her service. Her own pathway seemed easier as she served her parents. After many years, her parents passed away and that chapter of service was complete. Today, Charlene and her husband are serving a full-time mission in Kirtland, Ohio. Their example of service continues to inspire our family.

I know that it is vitally important that we teach our children the importance of service. In a world where selfishness and greed are accepted and almost encouraged, it is our responsibility as parents to provide opportunities for service. For children, service can be as simple as setting the table, reading a book to a sibling, or comforting a crying baby. When we see our children perform an act of service, we should acknowledge their actions and praise them. Talk about service with your children. Discuss how they felt as they were serving others.

Photo courtesy Sarah Steele.

Our family has befriended a dear elderly brother in our ward. Brother Pond is ninety-three years old. He joined the Church just four years ago. He has been a widower for many years, and his two sons live far away. My children enjoy visiting Brother Pond at his retirement home; they love to hear stories from his youth and look at the old photos he proudly displays on his bookshelf. Not long ago, after a visit with Brother Pond, our daughter Clara said, "I love visiting this place—I always have a happy feeling when we are here!" My husband and I took that opportunity to explain that the happy feeling she felt was the Holy Ghost testifying that what she just did was good! When we perform service, we are blessed with a warm happy feeling. Service enlightens our pathways.

Last is the bright light of *traditions*.

In the manual *Teaching, No Greater Call*, we learn that "one of the most powerful ways to establish righteous patterns of living is to create and maintain family traditions. Children feel secure in knowing that no matter what happens in their lives, certain events in their family will remain the same. President Ezra Taft Benson counseled: 'Foster wonderful family traditions which will bind you together eternally. In doing so, we can create a bit of heaven right here on earth within individual families.'"[10] There are bound to be disappointments and trials along our earthly pathway, but if we are able to create family traditions, we will have happy memories to sustain us through these difficult times.

Living our lives in the gospel light and creating strong spiritual traditions should be of the utmost importance. The scriptures testify of this.

In 3 John 1:4, it says, "I have no greater joy than to hear that my children walk in truth." In Proverbs 22:6, it says, "Train up a child in the way he should go; and when his is old, he will not depart from it." What kind of traditions do we have? Are they correct? Do they illuminate our pathways with gospel truth? Prayer, scripture study, fasting, paying our tithing, keeping the Sabbath day holy, and temple attendance are all worthy traditions. Not only are they traditions, but they are commandments from our Heavenly Father.

As we are raising our families, we need to make sure that these spiritual traditions are observed. Children thrive on routine. If prayer and scripture study are not part of your daily family routine, start now. It doesn't take long before righteous efforts become habits. In addition to morning and evening prayers, our family prays together in the car before driving any sizable distance. Saying a prayer is as much a habit as buckling our seat belts. If my husband or I by chance forget, one of the children will surely catch our mistake before we reach the end of the driveway. "Aren't we going to say a prayer?"

Keeping young children reverent and attentive during sacrament meeting can sometimes be a difficult task. In our family, we have observed several traditions or routines that have been extremely helpful in promoting reverence. Since they were babies, our children have known that nothing comes out of the diaper bag or scripture bags until after the passing of the sacrament is complete. Everyone in the family is expected to sing the hymns—and if they can't yet read they can at least have their hymnbooks open and "lead" the music. A family of two teenage boys in our ward has this tradition: The boys have the choice whether or not they sing the hymns. If they choose not to sing, they must perform a task at home before their dinner is served: They are required to write out by hand the words to all verses of the hymns sung in sacrament meeting. The boys quickly discovered that the easier choice was to sing!

My husband was eager to teach our young son the importance of priesthood responsibility. When James was just three, Jim began teaching him to "pass" the sacrament to our family. James reverently sits on the edge of the pew, and when the deacon comes to our row, James partakes of the sacrament and then takes the tray from the deacon and proceeds to pass the sacrament to each member of our family. I must admit that I was a bit worried about possible spills from a preschooler handling a tray of water cups. However, I'm pleased to report there has not been a single accident. James takes his responsibility very seriously. He is careful and reverent while passing the sacrament and always has a sweet little smile on his face as he serves our family and performs this sacred duty. Elder L. Tom Perry said, "If we will build righteous traditions in our families, the light of the gospel can grow ever brighter in our lives."[11]

Family traditions can also be fun and recreational. Oftentimes, traditions are created and observed for the sole purpose of spending time together, having fun, and creating memories. President Thomas S. Monson said, "We should make the most of today, of the here and now, doing all we can to provide pleasant memories for the future."[12] In the proclamation on the family, we learn that "successful marriages and families are maintained on [among other things] wholesome recreational activities."[13] Spending quality time together as a family builds unity and love.

Photo courtesy Sarah Steele.

My grandfather, President Monson, is a champion at creating fun family traditions. Some of my fondest childhood memories are those that were created by my grandparents. I remember singing Primary songs as we drove up the canyon, getting ice cream cones at Snelgroves, attending the circus, telling stories around the campfire, and fun-filled trips to Disneyland. As busy a man as President Monson is, he always finds time for his family. Every Sunday night, my grandma and grandpa would host a family gathering. These were simple, casual gatherings where we would all sit on the back porch, talk, and enjoy dessert. I loved Sunday nights and one of the greatest sacrifices of living in Connecticut is missing these still, ongoing Sunday gatherings.

Photo courtesy Sarah Steele.

As parents with a young family of our own, my husband and I have enjoyed creating our own fun traditions. We love making pancakes on Saturday mornings and then heading to the bike trail or going on a hike. We love celebrating the holidays with special homemade delicacies, and we love to decorate the house for birthdays. We love to go strawberry picking in the summer and apple picking in the fall. We love to create memories and spend time together as a family. One of President Monson's favorite quotations is from the Scottish poet, James Barrie, who declared, "God gave us memories, that we might have June roses in the December of our lives."[14] By creating traditions, we brighten our pathway and create lasting memories that will enlighten the paths of generations to come.

In closing, I'd like to refer to the final lines of the beautiful Primary song I began with: "I will work, and I will pray; / I will always walk in his way. / Then I will be happy on earth— / And in my home above."[15]

The journey along this earthly pathway is hard work, but our Heavenly Father loves us and wants us to be happy. He has provided many gospel lights to brighten our way. Knowledge, service, and traditions are just a few. It is my prayer that we might each "seek for God's light to direct us from birth."[16] Find a way that you can improve the light along your pathway. For a joyful path is the illuminated path.

Photo courtesy Shutterstock.

NOTES

1. Vanya Y. Watkins, "I Will Follow God's Plan," *Children's Songbook* (Salt Lake City: The Church of Jesus Christ of Latter-day Saints, 1989), 164–65.
2. Dieter F. Uchtdorf, "Forget Me Not," *Ensign*, November 2011, 122.
3. Henry B. Eyring, "Education for Real Life," *Ensign*, October 2002, 17.
4. Watkins, "I Will Follow God's Plan," 164–65.
5. Spencer W. Kimball, "The Role of Righteous Women," *Ensign*, November 1979, 102.
6. Gordon B. Hinckley, "Opposing Evil," *Ensign*, November 1975, 39.
7. Helen Silcott Dungan, "You Can Make the Pathway Bright," *Hymns of The Church of Jesus Christ of Latter-day Saints* (Salt Lake City: The Church of Jesus Christ of Latter-day Saints, 1985), no. 228.
8. Lorenzo Snow, in Conference Report, April 1899, 2–3.
9. Thomas S. Monson, "What Have I Done For Someone Today?" *Ensign*, November 2009, 85.
10. *Teaching, No Greater Call: A Resource Guide for Gospel Teaching* (Salt Lake City: The Church of Jesus Christ of Latter-day Saints, 1999), 135.

11. L. Tom Perry, "Family Traditions," *Ensign*, May 1990, 20.
12. Monson, "Finding Joy in the Journey," *Ensign*, November 2008, 85.
13. "The Family: A Proclamation to the World," *Ensign*, November 2010, 129.
14. James M. Barrie, in Monson, "How Firm a Foundation," *Ensign*, November 2006, 69.
15. Watkins, "I Will Follow God's Plan," 164–65.
16. Ibid.

Thoughts from the End of My Rope

Lynda M. Wilson

Three days before I was to give this presentation, I threw out my carefully prepared talk, including a PowerPoint presentation I was quite proud of, and started over from scratch.

Here's why.

I have been going through a challenge lately and this particular trial has left me feeling sort of desperate. I've been struggling with insomnia. I already contend with a number of chronic health problems that I normally am able to keep under control, but insomnia seems to be the straw that breaks the camel's back. Infections flare and life heads downhill. A whole chain of events is set in motion.

I start to dread going to bed. Tossing and turning on a spit from 3:30 a.m. until you finally give up and get out of bed at 6:00 a.m. saps your courage and strength. I know all about sleeping pills and I hate them. They are a devil's bargain. But finally you have to give in and start taking pills. It's not like the TV ads for Lunesta. You do not wake up like a happy butterfly. You wake up groggy with a headache. You plead with God for sleep—plain old ordinary sleep. No answer seems to come.

Then you remember that you're giving a talk at BYU Women's Conference on "Meeting the Challenges of Life with Strong Faith." You

---

Lynda M. Wilson is the author of The Innkeeper's Wife *and the coauthor of the scripture study blog* Sisters at the Well *(sistersatthewell.org). She is the wife of Elder Larry Y. Wilson of the Second Quorum of the Seventy, and they are the parents of four children and have seven grandchildren.*

wonder if you have anything to say. It feels like your back is against a wall.

So you scrap your old talk and write an entirely new one, entitled "Thoughts from the End of My Rope."

My presentation is from someone currently facing a challenge that requires faith. I'm in it, not through it. I'm also very aware that many of you are going through far worse things than chronic health challenges or insomnia. You need ways to tie knots in your own ropes to hang on to. With that perspective, here's what I do know about meeting life's difficulties with strong faith.

I want to start with Job. I think God put the book of Job in the scriptures so we would have a worst-case scenario, and so we would have it in black and white, from God, that trials do not necessarily come because of a person's sins or bad choices. They come because this is a fallen world and *God lets them come.* If God loves us—and I believe with all my heart that He does love us—and if He lets trials come, then living in a world where bad things happen to good people must ultimately be *for our good.* God must be able to bring good from the worst that life can hand us.

I like this quote: "You can't get away from suffering, that's the good news. For at the core of your most painful experiences—perhaps more than anywhere else—you will find the seeds of your awakening."[1]

So my first rule for life at the end of your rope is:

1. Trust God. No matter what happens, trust God. Trust that He is in control and that He is a just and a loving God. You not only *can* trust God; in fact, you *must* trust God. Who else can you trust?

When I was growing up, a family in our ward lost a daughter in a tragic car accident. They never came to church again. It was too much, they said. Contrast that attitude with Job's. When he was suffering terribly, when *all* his children were dead, he was covered with painful boils, he had lost all his earthly wealth, and his friends were accusing him of hidden sins that caused his trials, he said these remarkable words: "Though he slay me, yet will I trust . . . him" (Job 13:15). I think this is one of the greatest declarations of faith in all of scripture.

There was a time in the Lord's own ministry when many of His disciples turned back and quit following Him. It had become apparent that Jesus was not going to meet their expectations. He was not going to set up an earthly kingdom, not going to overthrow Rome, not going to continue to feed them free bread. And He said things they called "hard saying[s]," so they walked away. Do we do that? If the Lord doesn't meet our expectations and give us what we want, will we walk away, or will we give the answer that Peter gave when the Lord asked, "Will ye also go away?" Peter answered, "Lord, to whom [will] we go?" (John 6:60–68). Can we say, as Job said to his wife when she told him to "curse God, and die": "What? shall we receive good at the hand of God and not receive adversity also?" (Job 2:9–10). No matter what happens, don't stop trusting God.

My second rule for life at the end of your rope is:

2. Keep a channel open to God. He is there, but you have to open a way for him to communicate with you. Remember, he stands at the door and knocks. You have to do something that opens the door. There are two obvious ways: prayer and reading His word.

First, prayer—hard times require real prayer. Not trite phrases. I used to think praying was kind of like going in for an interview with a powerful official. The consequence of this bad thinking was that when I was weak, or had failed or sinned, I would avoid praying. I was only comfortable talking to God when I felt He would be proud of me. I told this to my little sister once. I said, "I have such a hard time praying when I have messed up." She was silent. "Don't you feel that way?" I asked her. "No," she replied. "If I've done something wrong I always pray as soon as I can, and I imagine Him saying, 'Oh Diana, I'm so glad you came to talk to me about this.' He's there to help us." It took me a while to learn that I'm not praying to impress God. I'm praying to someone who wants to help me with everything about my life, including my own fears and weakness.

My patriarchal blessing stated the obvious for me when I was twelve years old. It says, "Problems shall come into your life that will require great courage and strength. This courage and strength will be given to you as seek your Father in Heaven in prayer." I think for all of us the courage and strength we need does not come preinstalled at birth.

So pray—always. Even when there are no words, only tears. Get on your knees, which is to say humble yourself before the Lord every day. A key scripture in my life has been James 4:10: "Humble yourselves in the sight of the Lord, and he shall lift you up."

Then there is the channel of the iron rod.

Let me tell you about my good friend Vicki Ashton. As a young mother with many children, one of which was a new infant, she and her husband moved to Virginia. One day when they were still unpacking boxes, she went upstairs to nurse the baby and told the older children to watch the toddler. It happened that the new house had an indoor hot tub in the basement.

Well, someone's attention wandered just long enough for the toddler to climb into the hot tub. They found him floating there. He had not died, but he suffered severe brain damage. When he came home from the hospital he required around-the-clock care. Can you even imagine the grief and the guilt she felt? Being new to the area, she didn't even have a friend to turn to for support. Members of her new ward did rally round, and so my friend was able to get away one day for a trip to the temple. She sat in the celestial room pouring out her heart.

How can I do this, Lord? Where will I find the strength? What do I need to do to get through?

At some point as she prayed she heard a definite answer. The Lord spoke to her mind. *Read something from the scriptures every day.* She was incredulous. *That's it?* she replied. *Just read the scriptures every day?* It seemed an awfully simple answer to such big problems.

Yes, Vicki. You will be given the strength you need if you read my word every day. And now, many years later, I don't know anyone who bears a stronger testimony of the power of clinging to the iron rod through hard times than my friend Vicki Ashton.

Some of the crosses people are called upon to bear in this life seem unbearably heavy. My husband has a cousin, Anne, whose husband got a brain tumor pretty early in their marriage. He lived, but was disabled enough by the treatment that she became the breadwinner. Then she had a child with Down syndrome. Then their house burned down. Then they lost whatever money they had left in a bad investment. Then, believe it or not, *she* got a brain tumor. She beat it, though it affected her vision. In this last year, cancer has returned to her body, affecting many of her organs. Recently she had major surgery that left her with a colostomy.

I don't tell you her story to imply that your own troubles are small compared to hers. I tell it to you for two reasons. The first one is this:

Anne still has her faith in God intact. I think she would agree with Job: "Though he slay me, yet will I trust him."

The second reason is this: Even though God may not answer our prayers in the way we hoped He would, He still loves us and sends us reminders of that love when we need them. Just a few weeks ago, Anne was lying in her room in a rehabilitation facility when there came a little knock on the door, and a cheery voice asked, "May I come in?" It was President Thomas Monson, who happened to be in the hospital visiting someone else. He gave her a sweet blessing and visited with her. In fact, he spent a whole hour with her, a tender mercy to remind a faithful Latter-day Saint woman how much God loved her.

God may not always take away the awful thing, but He lets you know He's there and that He loves you.

That is my third rule for hanging on when you're at the end of your rope:

3. God sends love notes, even in the worst of times. Look for them. A friend once gave me some very good advice. She said, "Ask God to show you how He feels about you." What a wonderful prayer to pray!

Let me tell you about Martha and Steve, and how, in the midst of the awful trial of losing a child, God showed them how he felt about them. Their daughter Sarah was killed in an automobile accident when she was eighteen. She'd been one of my daughter's closest friends. She was a wonderful, vivacious young woman, full of faith. She was in a car with cousins going to a wedding. There was an accident. Sarah's seat belt was broken and she was thrown from the car and killed instantly. No one else was even hurt.

As Sarah's funeral approached, her parents had to go through all the preparations, including choosing a casket. Martha was discouraged. The caskets were all lined the way caskets are, with shiny pleated satin. But this just wasn't her daughter. Some might say it was a trivial thing, but it broke her mother's heart to think of putting Sarah in one of those stuffy pink or white satin boxes. So she couldn't bring herself to choose.

The funeral director saw her dismay. "There is one other casket," he said. "It's quite different. We were going to send it back because we hadn't ordered it and don't know why the casket company sent it. It's lined with a quilt. Would you like to see it?" Well now, Sarah's mother, Martha, was a quilter, the best one in our whole stake. Yes, she said, she would like to see it. This casket was lined with a peach-and-cream-colored patchwork quilt. Those were the very colors of Sarah's bedroom. Martha wept. She would be able to wrap her daughter in that quilt. God can't always take away the pain. But He has ways of being with us in the pain.

Which brings me to my fourth rule for hanging on at the end of your rope:

4. Realize that Jesus Christ knows your suffering intimately. He felt it—all of it—and so can be with you every step of the way. Cling to that; cling to the Atonement.

Twenty-six years ago, my brother, who was in his early twenties and suffering from schizophrenia that I believe was induced by all the drugs he had taken, killed his wife and child and then himself. My sister was closer to him than I had been. I left for college when he was only six. But their relationship had been a close one and she was nearly devastated with grief. One night she couldn't sleep for the sorrow of it all and slipped out of bed onto her knees. *Oh Father,* she prayed. *Please take this crushing grief away. I can't bear it.* And then she heard this answer.

"I can't do that, my child. Grieving is part of living in this world. But I promise you, I will be with you through it all."

Jesus Christ promised his followers, "I will never leave you or forsake you" (see Hebrews 13:5). Sometimes it is hard to believe that He is really there and knows what we're going through, but I believe He does know.

It says in Psalm 61, "When my heart is overwhelmed, lead me to the Rock that is higher than I" (Psalm 61:2). Jesus Christ is the Rock that is higher than we are, and yet, He is also the one who suffered Himself, going below all things so that there is nothing He can't understand or relate to. That is the power of His Atonement.

The Apostle Paul spoke of entering into "the fellowship of his sufferings" (Philippians 3:10). In other words, Paul let his own hardships—the beatings, stonings, shipwrecks, imprisonments, hunger, fatigue, rejection—he let all of it bring him into closer fellowship with the Savior, who had Himself suffered so greatly. Paul regarded his own suffering as a way to relate to what the Lord had done for him.

This can seem like a hard doctrine. We don't want to hear that suffering can be good for us. But I have discovered that even more than wanting to be free of pain, we want our trials and sufferings to have *meaning.* We don't want to feel that we are helpless bugs and the universe is a big bully pulling off our wings. Albert Einstein has been quoted as saying, "The most important question we can ask in this life is: Is this universe a friendly place?" Because of the Atonement of Jesus Christ, the answer is yes.

A beloved stake president of mine when I was growing up, Joseph Hilton, had occasion to put this to the test. He came down with bone cancer, one of the most painful of all cancers because your bone marrow grows too fast and pushes outward on all your bones. One day he lay in his darkened bedroom in excruciating physical pain until finally he cried out: "Oh Lord, I cannot bear this pain. Take it away, I beg you, or take my life." He said that at that moment, he felt as if the stopper on a drain had been pulled out from the bottom of his feet, and the pain began to drain away, from the top of his head, through his body, and out his feet. He just lay there in happy shock—pain free. But after a time, he heard the voice of the Lord whisper, "I hear you, my son, but my ways are not your ways." Then, very slowly, the pain returned.

When we are in pain, we must never let ourselves believe that somehow God isn't aware or doesn't love us or is indifferent to our suffering. That is simply never true. If we can't hold on to anything else, we can remember that "His ways are not our ways," and we can decide to trust His love.

President Hilton's cancer went into remission, and he had several more years of active life. His wife always said that he was a changed man after his experience of suffering with cancer. He had always been a righteous man, a very straight-arrow type of guy. After the cancer he was softer. He cried easily and was more inclined to forgive the weaknesses of others.

When my own son was seven months old he had to go to the pediatrician for a procedure to redo his circumcision because the skin at one point had grown back together. It was an awful experience. His arms and legs were strapped down to a table and the whole time they were working on him he was wailing hysterically and staring right at my face, as if he were saying, "You're my mother. Why are you letting them do this to me? Don't you love me?"

Of course I loved him, but I had to let him go through an experience that was ultimately for his good.

Twenty-five years later I picked up the phone late one night and heard that same son wailing once more. He finally was able to speak, and said, "She's gone. The baby's dead. There's no heartbeat." Their first child, a baby girl named Reese, was stillborn at eight months. Her little body was beautiful and perfect. We never knew why she died.

Over the next few days and weeks I recognized that he was going through a familiar process. "You're my Father. Why have you let this happen to us? Don't you love us?" After a wrestle with himself, much prayer, and a blessing from his father, he came to faith, and was able to put himself in the hands of the Great Physician.

My fifth and last principle for hanging on at the end of your rope is:

5. Have gratitude for what you do have. I have learned to look for the ways that the Lord is blessing me, even when a particular trial isn't going away. Gratitude for what you do have is a great antidote for panic and grief over what you don't have.

Having gratitude isn't easy. I can remember when I used to complain about things as a girl, my grandmother would say in a cheery voice, "Count your blessings." This used to annoy the heck out of me. Complaining, wallowing in your misery, and playing the part of a victim can feel good in a carnal sort of way. But I want to tell you now about a girl I met once, who did a lot to cure me of my moaning and griping disease.

I call her the Madonna of the Wheelchair because, unfortunately, I don't know her name. If anyone in this life ever had the right to complain it was this young woman. When I was in my early twenties, I worked part-time at American Fork Training School as a caregiver while attending Brigham Young University. This large residential facility housed people with all degrees of mental and physical disabilities.

There was a little chapel on the campus where volunteers held LDS services. One fast Sunday I was there with my charges, and this young woman—she was probably about my age—was pushed in in a wheelchair. She was tied into her chair and had socks on her hands. She appeared to have cerebral palsy. Because it was fast Sunday, the priesthood holder conducting asked if anyone wanted to bear his or her testimony.

She obviously did. She became very animated as if trying to raise her hand. Her speech was labored and very difficult to understand. But her thoughts were perfectly cogent.

What she said was simple: "I want to bear my testimony. Father in Heaven . . . thank you for all our blessings. This world thinks we don't have much, but they don't know. I know. Thank you so much Father, for all that you have given us."

That was all. She bore this simple testimony to bear witness to the faith she had in her Heavenly Father and to say thank you for her life. After she finished she had a huge smile on her face and I realized with astonishment that she was happy.

It was important to her to bear a public testimony so that others would know how she felt about her own life. She wanted us to know she was not bitter that her mind was imprisoned in a body like that, and she was not angry that her family had left her in this place. She was *grateful*!

I think the Lord allowed me to witness her testimony that day so that I could honor her faith by sharing it with others. Perhaps, like Paul, she had entered into the fellowship of Christ's sufferings. She had used her pain to grow very close to the Savior and His Spirit, and she was grateful for that fellowship. How amazing is that? I hope she and I meet again someday.

If we use our own reasoning to try and figure out the spiritual accounting inherent in this earth life we will fail miserably. We see so little of the true reality. I remember hearing of a remark made by an old woman who came finally to live in Utah after thirty years of life as a Latter-day Saint behind the Iron Curtain. When asked if she liked her new life here she said, yes, of course, but added, "It's odd though. I haven't talked to one person yet who has seen an angel." Have we become, then, spiritually spoiled by the abundance in our lives? Do we lose the spiritual privileges that might have been ours because of this?

When our trials come, we need to be like the little child of Mosiah 3:19, "submissive, meek, humble, patient, full of love, willing to submit to all things whatsoever the father seeth fit to inflict upon us, even as a child doth submit to his father." That is the ultimate knot in the end of the rope.

Actually, it's not a rope we hang on to, is it? It's a hand. Someone is reaching down from above and holding us tightly in a Father's firm grip, and He won't let us go as long as we continue to trust in Him.

So, after these last few weeks struggling with insomnia, I finally asked myself, *What if you never again in your life have a good night's sleep? What if the health flare-ups become constant?* And this is what I've decided: I'll keep looking for answers but I don't need to panic. With the Lord's help I can do whatever I need to do.

I can trust God. I can keep open the channels of communication with Him. I can look for the tender mercies that remind me He loves me even if this particular problem doesn't go away. I can cling to the Atonement, knowing that Christ suffered all things for us so that He could be with us in our own suffering. And finally, I can be grateful, focusing my vision on all that I do have, starting with my sure knowledge that I am God's beloved child and that the gospel path is the way back home.

The sorrows of our lives are a gift—the seeds of our awakening—if only we can see them that way. The Germans have a cool word for a God-ordained trial. The word is *Heimsuchung.* It literally means "visitation." In this view, when trials come, the Lord has literally visited us. It is up to us to take advantage of that visit, and enter into fellowship with Him through our suffering.

I testify that earth has no sorrow that heaven cannot heal. I testify that when our heart is overwhelmed, Christ is the Rock that is higher than we are.

NOTE

1. Pema Chodron, *Noble Heart: A Self-Guided Retreat on Befriending Your Obstacles* (Louisville, CO: Sounds True Inc., 1998), audiobook.

Holding On to the Iron Rod Even When You Can't See the Tree of Life

Brent L. Top

The scriptural theme for this session of Women's Conference comes from Daniel 3:17–18. You remember the story. If you are like me, then your mother probably shared this Bible story with you even before you were able to read. It is the story of Shadrach, Meshach, and Abed-nego, who refuse to worship the pagan gods of the Babylonians and are cast into the fiery furnace by King Nebuchadnezzar. When the death sentence is pronounced upon them, they respond: "If it be so, our God whom we serve is able to deliver us from the burning fiery furnace, and he will deliver us out thine hand, O king. *But if not,* be it known unto thee, O king, that we will not serve thy gods, nor worship the golden image which thou has set up" (Daniel 3:17–18; emphasis added).

This passage dramatically illustrates the faith of true disciples—a belief that God knows us personally and is aware of our unique circumstances, our desperate needs, and the desires of our hearts. It is the absolute assurance that God indeed has power to do something—anything to rescue us, strengthen us, save us! It is the next phrase, however, that is most profound—"*but if not.*" This reminds us that devoted, faith-filled

---

Brent L. Top served in the Denmark Copenhagen Mission. He received his bachelor's, master's, and PhD degrees from Brigham Young University. He is a professor of Church history and doctrine at BYU, and currently chair of that department. He served as president of the Illinois Peoria Mission from 2004–2007, and serves as president of the Pleasant Grove East Stake. He and his wife, Wendy, are the parents of four children.

disciples not only *trust* in God's power, *hope* that He will mercifully intervene in our behalf, but also *submit* to His will *even if* things aren't going to turn out the way we hope.

While Shadrach, Meshach, and Abed-nego are ancient scriptural examples of supreme faith and hope in God's almighty power and willing submission to His will, I have seen modern examples of the same that have inspired me and blessed my life. Let me share with you one.

As a mission president I often received phone calls from family members of our missionaries or their priesthood leaders back at home informing me of emergencies or deaths in the family. It became my responsibility then to discuss these matters with the missionaries and to help them deal with the challenges and to provide loving support. On one occasion an elder was told that his mother had been diagnosed with a very aggressive form of cancer. The doctors and family, however, were hopeful of, if not a full recovery, at least many more years of life. The family assured their missionary that things would be all right. At every interview I had with him, I would inquire how his mother was doing. He was always so upbeat and positive, full of faith that God could heal her or at least prolong her life. I can only imagine how fervent his prayers were in behalf of his mother, father, and family. No doubt those prayers included that familiar phrase, "Thy will be done." I have learned in my life that it is easier to say it than to really mean it.

The "but if not" moment came for this young missionary much, much sooner than he or I expected. His mother's condition deteriorated quickly. Her death was sudden and shocking. I had the dreaded task of informing him that his mother, whom he had so fervently prayed for and hoped for a miracle for, had been taken home. I tried my best to comfort and console him, but my words seemed pretty shallow at the moment.

In the months that followed, I was inspired by how this young man dealt with this loss and heartache. Things clearly had not worked out the way he hoped and prayed for. How would he respond? Would it shake his faith in the Lord and his commitment to the kingdom? Not for a moment did he consider cutting his mission short and going home. Not for a moment did his pace slacken nor did his work suffer. In fact, he worked harder, and in many ways, was even more effective as a missionary. I was worried that he was in denial, suppressing his true feelings. There was a concern that he hadn't dealt with his grief and that he would eventually crash and burn. Yet I didn't see evidence of any of that. There was no apparent bitterness, no expressions of anger, no questioning God or doubting His power or love. He bore this challenge with incredible strength and grace. How was he able to do it?

Several months after we returned from our mission, Sister Top and I attended the sacrament meeting where this remarkable young man reported his mission. We saw a stark contrast between this spiritually mature, confident, powerful missionary and the fearful, struggling nineteen-year-old who had come to our mission two years previously. As he spoke of his mother's death and how he dealt with it, he made a simple observation that powerfully affected me. He said, "I held on to the iron rod even when I could not see the tree of life."

I really like that thought; it is more profound than my young missionary knew. The image his statement creates in my mind corresponds with some interesting phrases used by Nephi in his scriptural accounts of his father's dream and his own vision of the same. After Lehi had partaken of the fruit of the tree—the fruit he described as "desirable above all other fruit" that filled his soul "with exceedingly great joy"—he beckoned to his family that they come also partake (1 Nephi 8:12). I find it interesting that in verse 14, Lehi tells us that even his wife, Sariah, and faithful sons Nephi and Sam hesitated—"and they stood as if they knew not whither they should go" (1 Nephi 8:14). Lehi had to coach, coax, and cajole them forward "with a loud voice" (1 Nephi 8:15). Isn't that phrase interesting? Why did he have to use a "loud voice"? Could it be possible that (1) the tree was a long way away, or (2) they couldn't see either Lehi or the tree, or (3) both? Could it be that they were in a desert sandstorm with wind howling in their ears and sand beating against their faces? Is it possible that they could only hear the distant voice of Father Lehi as they viewed the never-before-seen rod of iron leading to an unknown, never-before-encountered destination? Yet they trusted and moved forward.

In contrast, Laman and Lemuel "would not come"—even when they also heard their father's voice and beheld the iron rod (1 Nephi 8:18). Why not? Was it because they didn't like fruit? No, I don't think that was it. I think it was because what they did see clouded what they couldn't see. They couldn't see the tree, but they did see a "strait and narrow path"

(1 Nephi 8:20), a river of filthy water in which many who lost their way were drowned (see 1 Nephi 8:32; 12:16), "mists of darkness" that were so oppressive and consuming that many who "commenced in the path did lose their way, that they wandered off and were lost" (1 Nephi 8:23). As if that were not enough to scare the dickens out of them, there was the spacious field with crisscrossing paths going in every direction, and the great and spacious building and its finely adorned inhabitants "in the attitude of mocking and pointing their fingers toward those who had come at and were partaking of the fruit" (1 Nephi 8:27).

President Boyd K. Packer has often recounted the story of counsel he received shortly after he was called to be a General Authority. He had encountered what he considered to be an insurmountable obstacle. He saw no way around it except to give up and go a different direction. When he reported this to Elder Harold B. Lee, Brother Lee said: "'Do you know what is wrong with you—you always want to see the end from the beginning.'

"I replied quietly that I wanted to see at least a few steps ahead. He answered by quoting from the sixth verse of the twelfth chapter of Ether: 'Wherefore, dispute not because ye see not, for ye have no witness until after the trial of your faith.'

"And then he added, 'My boy, you must learn to walk to the edge of the light, and perhaps a few steps into the darkness, and you will find that the light will appear and move ahead of you.'

"And so it has—but only as we walked to the edge of the light."[1]

Each of us, like Sariah, Nephi, and Sam, will have to walk into the darkness at times in our lives—not knowing what is over the next hill, but holding on to the iron rod and listening for the sometimes distant voice beckoning us onward. Sometimes the mists of darkness will engulf us and spiritual or emotional sandstorms will beat against us and threaten our very grip on the iron rod. It is at that very moment—our customized "but if not" moment—that faith and holding on becomes a matter of life and death.

One person who faced this very dilemma was the British author C. S. Lewis. A convert to Christianity, Lewis became one of the faith's most ardent and articulate defenders. Amidst the gathering storm clouds of World War II and the anxiety and worry that it brought, C. S. Lewis was asked to deliver lectures of hope and understanding to British airmen preparing to enter combat. And then, owing to the success of these lectures, Lewis was invited to write a book about "the problem of pain" in the world. Published in 1940, *The Problem of Pain* made C. S. Lewis famous worldwide. Lewis was a master at taking a complex philosophical or theological issue and, with relevant analogies and simple language, making it easy to understand. He had great answers for life's difficult questions. With the success of *The Problem of Pain,* Lewis was invited to deliver a weekly radio lecture on the BBC explaining and defending the tenets of Christianity. These popular lectures, given from 1942 to 1944, were later published in a book entitled *Mere Christianity.* Millions of people around the world have been instructed and inspired by these works.

In *The Problem of Pain,* Lewis stated that adversity is God's "megaphone to rouse a deaf world."[2] He taught that suffering and sorrow, trials and tribulations can turn men to God. "Pain insists on being attended to," Lewis wrote. "God whispers to us in our pleasures, speaks in our conscience, but shouts in our pains."[3] He further explained:

> God, who made us, knows what we are and that our happiness lies in Him. Yet we will not see it in Him as long as He leaves us any other resort where it can even plausibly be looked for. While what we call "our own life" remains agreeable we will not surrender it to Him. What then can God do in our interests but to make "our own life" less agreeable to us, and take away the plausible sources of false happiness? It is just here, where God's providence seems at first to be most cruel, that the Divine humility, the stooping down of the Highest, most deserves praise.[4]

In 1940, C. S. Lewis could not have known that his eloquent explanations, his carefully reasoned responses to the problem of pain in the world—his own words that had instructed and inspired so many around the world—would become to him, as he himself explained, a "matter of life and death." In 1956, the avowed bachelor met and married an American divorcee named Joy Davidman Gresham. Perhaps Lewis himself was surprised by the joy and fulfillment that married life provided him. "I never expected to have in my sixties," he said to a friend, "the happiness that passed me by in my twenties."[5] Just a few months after their marriage, it was discovered that Joy had cancer. The next few years were filled with surgeries and treatments and pains along with moments of supreme happiness. Joy died in July 1960 and the grieving C. S. Lewis—he who always had had great answers and comforting counsel—"was unable even to think or to write or to pray."[6] Out of this deeply personal clash between the "head knowledge" that he had expounded twenty years previously and the "experiential knowledge" he was painfully acquiring in his profound grief came one of his most important works. *A Grief Observed* was his attempt to describe the pain, loss, and loneliness he experienced and to understand the meaning of it all. Twenty years earlier, Lewis had the answers, but now in his deepest, darkest moments he had questions—even doubts. "Where is God?" he wrote.

> When you are happy, so happy that you have no sense of needing Him, so happy that you are tempted to feel His claims upon you as an interruption, if you remember yourself and turn to Him with gratitude and praise, you will be—or so it feels—welcomed with open arms. But you go to Him when your need is desperate, when all other help is vain, and what do you find? A door slammed in your face and a sound of bolting and double bolting on the inside. After that, silence. You may as well turn away. The longer you wait, the more emphatic the silence will become. There are no lights in the windows. It might be an empty house. Was it ever inhabited? It seemed so once. And that seeming was as strong as this. What can this mean? Why is [God] so present a commander in our time of prosperity and so very absent a help in time of trouble?[7]

Lewis's next statement shows us that he was learning more profound answers and receiving more abiding comfort through his crucible of experience than he had from merely theorizing, book reading, or even book writing. He was forced to examine whether his current convictions matched his earlier eloquent words.

> You never know how much you really believe anything until its truth or falsehood becomes a matter of life and death to you. It is easy to say you believe a rope to be strong and sound as long as you are merely using it to cord a box. But suppose you had to hang by that rope over a precipice. Wouldn't you then first discover how much you really trusted it? . . . Only a real risk tests the reality of belief.
>
> . . . Nothing less will shake a man—or at any rate a man like me—out of his merely verbal thinking and his merely notional beliefs. He has to be knocked silly before he comes to his senses.[8]

It is in these moments when we are "knocked silly"—when we have walked not only a few steps into the darkness, but also when we are surrounded by the "mists of darkness" and cannot see the tree of life—that holding on may be not only the most important thing we can do, but the only thing. Only when we hang by the thread of our convictions do we find out what we really believe, to whom we are really loyal, and what spiritual substance really fills our souls.

After a long while of stumbling in the dark abyss of his own personal grief, C. S. Lewis began to notice the light. He began to discern in his own life what we know from modern revelation: "After much tribulation come the blessings" (D&C 58:4). As he began his journey out of the darkness of doubt, he wrote:

> You can't see anything properly while your eyes are blurred with tears. You can't in most things get what you want if you want it too desperately: and you can't get the best out of it. . . . And so perhaps with God. I have gradually been coming to feel that the door is no longer shut and bolted. Was it my own frantic need that slammed it in my face? The time where there is nothing at all in your soul except a cry for help may be just the time when God can't give it to you: you are like a drowning man who can't be helped because he clutches and grabs. Perhaps your own reiterated cries deafen you to the voice you hoped to hear.[9]

So what does it all mean? How do we get from the "knocked silly" point—the "Why me? Why this? Why now?" point—to the "but if not . . . I will not give up or give in" point? How do we get to the point where we can say to the Lord, "Thy will be done" and really mean it and submit to it?

Not long before his death, in a book entitled *Letters to Malcolm: Chiefly on Prayer,* C. S. Lewis commented on what the phrase "Thy will be done" had come to mean to him.

> At first I took it exclusively as an act of submission, attempting to do with it what Our Lord did in Gethsemane. I thought of God's will purely as something that would come upon me, something of which I should be patient. And I also thought of it as a will which would be embodied in pains and disappointments. Not, to be sure, that I supposed God's will for me to consist entirely of disagreeables. But I thought it was only the disagreeables that called for the preliminary submission—the agreeables could look after themselves for the present. When they turned up, one could give thanks.
>
> This interpretation is, I expect, the commonest. And so it must be. And such are the miseries of human life that must often fill our whole mind. But at other times other meanings can be added. So I added one more. . . .

He then goes on to explain what submitting to the will of God—however painful, however disappointing, and however long such pains and disappointments may continue—had come to mean to him after he had walked in the "mists of darkness."

> "Thy will be done." But a great deal of it is to be done by God's creatures; including me. The petition, then, is not merely that I may patiently suffer God's will but also that I may vigorously do it. I must be an agent as well as a patient. I am asking that I may be *enabled* to do it. In the long run I am asking to be given "the same mind which was also in Christ."
>
> Taken this way, I find the words have a more regular daily

> application. For there isn't always—or we don't always have reason to suspect that there is—some great affliction looming in the near future, but there are always duties to be done; usually for me, neglected duties to be caught up with. "Thy will be *done*—by me—*now*" brings one back to brass tacks.[10]

There it is. There is the answer—"duties to be done," "neglected duties to be caught up with." That is what Lehi and Nephi characterized as holding on to the iron rod—"multitudes pressing forward; and they came and caught hold of the end of the rod of iron; and they did press their way forward, *continually holding fast to the rod of iron*, until they came forth and fell down and partook of the fruit of the tree" (1 Nephi 8:30; emphasis added). That phrase, "continually holding fast," reminds us that submitting to the will of God isn't just needed during the sporadic seasons of our suffering, but continually—day by day, hour by hour. It is found in every prayer that we offer, every time we read scriptures—even if it is just a verse or a chapter and even if we don't fully understand everything we read. It is there every time we worthily partake of the sacrament. It is found in every temple session we attend, every act of service that we give, every expression of kindness and gratitude, every smile we share. "Holding fast" is being obedient and trying to do good, be good, and desiring to be a little better. It is loving more and being willing to feel love—especially His love. Nephi taught that "whoso would hearken unto the word of God, and would hold fast unto it, they would never perish; neither could the temptations and the fiery darts of the adversary overpower them unto blindness, to lead them away to destruction" (1 Nephi 15:24).

It is my hope and my prayer for you and for me that we will indeed daily hold on to the iron rod even when we can't see the Tree of Life. That is what my missionary did in his deepest sorrow. He got up each day and prayed and studied and worked. Undoubtedly there were many tears, but he kept going. He kept "pressing forward"—some days more rapidly than others—but he held on to the iron rod. Holding fast rarely requires the sensational, but it always requires the steady. Elder B. H. Roberts explained:

> There is no one great thing that man can do and then do no more and obtain salvation. . . . It is by resisting a temptation today, overcoming a weakness tomorrow, forsaking evil associations the next day, and thus day by day, month after month, year after year, pruning, restraining and weeding out that which is evil in the disposition, that the character is purged of its imperfections. . . .
>
> [We] must cultivate noble sentiments by performing noble deeds—not great ones, necessarily, for opportunity to do what the world esteems great things, comes but seldom to men in the ordinary walks of life; but noble deeds may be done every day; and every such deed performed with an eye single to the glory of God, draws one that much nearer into harmony with Deity.[11]

May we hold fast and press forward in our happy times and in our "but if not" moments. I bear testimony that God lives. He is mindful of you and me. He loves us with a perfect love. I bear witness that like Shadrach, Meshach and Abed-nego, the Son of Man will be with us in whatever our fiery furnace.

Notes

1. Boyd K. Packer, *Mine Errand from the Lord* (Salt Lake City: Deseret Book, 2008), 62.
2. C. S. Lewis, *The Problem of Pain* (New York: Macmillan, 1962), 93.
3. Ibid.
4. Ibid., 85–86.
5. Lewis, in *The C. S. Lewis Reader's Encyclopedia* (Grand Rapids, MI: Zondervan, 1998), 60.
6. Ibid., 62.
7. Lewis, *A Grief Observed* (New York: Bantam Books, 1961), 4–5.
8. Ibid., 25, 43.
9. Ibid., 63–64.
10. C. S. Lewis, *Letters to Malcolm: Chiefly on Prayer* (New York: Harcourt, Brace and Company, 1992), 25–26.
11. B. H. Roberts, *The Gospel: An Exposition of Its First Principles; and Man's Relationship to Diety, Third Edition* (Salt Lake City: The Deseret News, 1901), 208–9.

I Can Do Hard Things: Lessons from the Old Testament

Terry B. Ball

I am thankful for the opportunity to speak at Women's Conference this year. It is not often I have the occasion to speak to such an important and influential group. I hope I will do justice to the privilege. I have been asked to speak to the theme of "I can do hard things." As I pondered the topic I decided to make a list of the hard things women are regularly asked to do. As I was making the list I felt humbled and awed by the multitude and magnitude of what is asked of you. For example, if you are a typical homemaker your list of duties on any given day might include any or all of the following jobs: wife, mother, nutritionist, cook, waitress, busboy, dishwasher, custodian, seamstress, wardrobe manager, teacher, counselor, dating and marriage therapist, fashion advisor, financial planner, acquisitions and matériel controller, transportation engineer, accountant, taxi driver, motivational speaker, spiritual counselor, health advisor, nurse, dispute mediator, coach, health inspector, laundry coordinator, landscaper, recreation manager, home repair supervisor, security manager, emergency preparedness coordinator, cheerleader, and homework consultant. And these are just some of the routine expectations.

Throughout your lives there will be occasions when you may be faced with unexpected and extraordinary tasks as well, such as dealing with

---

Terry B. Ball is a professor of ancient scripture at Brigham Young University. He received his bachelor's, master's, and PhD degrees from BYU. He has taught and traveled extensively in the Holy Land, including teaching at the BYU Jerusalem Center for Near Eastern Studies. He and his wife, DeAnna, have six children.

debilitating health issues for yourself or loved ones, financial setbacks, wayward loved ones, demanding church and civic responsibilities, natural disasters, marriage challenges, and pregnancy. I think it is amazing that we hope you will be able to do all of this, and so much more, with a pleasant, charming, efficient, and unflappable demeanor. What is even more surprising to me is how very often you actually manage it.

You are truly marvelous works and wonders. Consequently, as a man, I feel somewhat underqualified for this speaking assignment. Indeed, it has been a hard thing for me to think of anything I could teach you about how to do hard things. As I studied and prayed about the topic I was eventually drawn to three Old Testament figures who were asked to do extremely hard things. I believe their experiences and examples can teach us much about how to accomplish the difficult tasks we face during mortality.

The first I would like to consider is Moses. As you remember, at the age of forty, after being raised in the luxury of Pharaoh's household, he fled to the stark wilderness of Sinai (see Exodus 2:15). There he met and married Zipporah the daughter of Jethro or Reuel, the high priest of Midian, from whom he received the Melchizedek Priesthood (see Exodus 2:16–22; D&C 84:6–7). He spent the next forty years of his life as a simple shepherd scratching out an existence in that hostile desert.

I suppose that as Moses grew older he concluded that he would spend the remainder of his days shepherding his flocks, and was likely content with that life, but God had other plans. When Moses was a full eighty years of age, well past retirement by our standards, the Lord asked him to do a very hard thing. We are told that as he was herding his sheep in the "backside of the desert" at Mount Horeb he turned aside to see a strange sight—a bush that was burning but not consumed. (I have been to the Sinai desert—it is a truly bleak and barren place. Each time I have been there I have thought to myself Moses may have "turned aside" simply because he saw a bush!) God spoke to Moses "out of the midst of the bush," and declared, "Behold, the cry of the children of Israel is come unto me: and I have also seen the oppression wherewith the Egyptians oppress them. Come now therefore, and I will send thee unto Pharaoh, that thou mayest bring forth my people the children of Israel out of Egypt" (Exodus 3:9–10).

We can imagine how overwhelmed Moses must have felt at being given such an assignment. Egypt was a powerful and fearsome nation. In spite of his royal upbringing Moses was now a relatively poor, humble, geriatric shepherd. He had fled from Egypt forty years earlier, and considering the circumstances under which he left, the Egyptian leaders likely would not be glad to see him. Pharaoh certainly would not be pleased to hear a demand to free his Israelite slaves, and could well order Moses' immediate execution just for asking. Obviously overwhelmed by what the Lord was asking of him, Moses begged, "Who am I, that I should go unto Pharaoh, and that I should bring forth the children of Israel out of Egypt?" (Exodus 3:11). In other words, Moses seems to be asking, "Why me? Don't you have someone more qualified? I don't have the talent and ability to do such a thing. I'm so inadequate! Why me?" I suspect some of us have had similar feelings when asked to accept a challenging church calling or accomplish some difficult assignment.

I have come to appreciate the principle taught by the Lord's simple and direct response to Moses' concerns. As Moses expressed his worries about his inadequacies, the Lord assured him, "Certainly, I will be with thee" (Exodus 3:12). There is a sermon in that simple sentence. As Moses claims he is inadequate for the job, the Lord's response seems to say to him, "Well, of course you are inadequate, but that is not important. This work will be accomplished by my power, not yours. You may be inadequate, but I am not, and certainly, I will be with thee!" Moses was to be God's instrument for the work, but God would guide and empower the instrument. From that exchange, Moses learned that our Heavenly Father is more concerned about our availability than our capabilities. As President Thomas S. Monson frequently reminds us, "Whom the Lord calls, the Lord qualifies."[1] If we will make ourselves available to do God's work, he will make us capable.

Moses subsequently raised another concern: "But, behold, they will not believe me, nor hearken unto my voice" (Exodus 4:1). The prophet was clearly afraid of failure. God taught him another valuable lesson about facing "hard things" in the conversation that followed. He asked Moses: "What is that in thine hand? And he said, A rod. And he said, Cast it on the ground. And he cast it on the ground, and it became a serpent; and Moses fled from before it. And the Lord said unto Moses, Put forth thine hand, and take it by the tail. And he put forth his hand, and caught it, and it became a rod in his hand" (Exodus 4:2–4).

The Lord went on to explain that this act was to be the first of several signs Moses was to show the people to convince them he was sent by God, but there seems to be another teaching purpose in the demonstration as well. Moses was so frightened by the serpent that he fled from it. That serpent can be understood to have represented all of Moses' fears, and we can hardly blame Moses for wanting to flee. Imagine the courage it took for Moses to trust the Lord's instructions enough to return to the serpent, reach down, and snatch it by the tail—certainly a hard thing for him to do. Imagine the relief Moses must have felt when the venomous creature again became a rod in his hand. From this experience, Moses was assured that if he would trust God and follow His commands exactly—if he would get ahold of his fears, then God could and would help him manage those fears. He would help him do hard things.

Nearly a thousand years later another prophet, Jeremiah, a humble priest from Anatoth, would be taught this same lesson. Few of us will experience as much hardship and rejection as did Jeremiah. He was a prophet to the kingdom Judah at a time when the nation was a vassal state to the Babylonian Empire. Egypt had been encouraging Judah to rebel against Babylonian vassalage with the promise that they would support Judah in the rebellion. History reveals that the Egyptians' encouragement was self-serving. They sought to keep Babylon away from their own borders by keeping the Babylonian armies preoccupied with rebellion in Judah. What little and temporary support Egypt did send when Judah rebelled against Babylon failed to save the nation. The Lord tried to warn Judah of Egypt's duplicity through Jeremiah. The prophet pleaded with his people to not trust Egypt or rebel against Babylon but to trust in God for deliverance (see Jeremiah 37–39). For those warnings, Jeremiah was viewed as a traitor and a threat to national security. His own townspeople and kinsmen of Anatoth denounced him and threatened to kill him for prophesying in the name of the Lord (see Jeremiah 11:21). The governor of his fellow priests had him beaten and placed in stocks for the public to deride (see Jeremiah 20:1–6). The king personally cut up Jeremiah's written prophecy and threw it in the fire, and later, at the request of the military, had the prophet thrown into a dungeon pit to wallow in the mire (see Jeremiah 36:22–26; 38:4–6). Indeed, all the people sought his life for declaring the word of God (see Jeremiah 26:8–9).

As Jeremiah faced these hardships he likely found strength and resolve by reflecting on the lessons he learned when the Lord first called him to do hard things, saying: "Before I formed thee in the belly I knew thee; and before thou camest forth out of the womb I sanctified thee, and I ordained thee a prophet unto the nations" (Jeremiah 1:5). Startled and feeling overwhelmed and inadequate for such a commission, Jeremiah protested: "Ah, Lord God! behold, I cannot speak: for I am a child" (Jeremiah 1:6).

There is a sense of censure as the Lord responded to his protest: "Say not, I am a child: for thou shalt go to all that I shall send thee, and whatsoever I command thee thou shalt speak" (Jeremiah 1:7). Then, as he had done with Moses, God assured the insecure prophet, "Be not afraid of their faces: for I am with thee" (Jeremiah 1:8). Once again the Lord teaches that when asked to do hard things we need to trust Him, set aside our fears, keep His commandments, and let God work through us. When we make ourselves available, God will be with us and make us capable.

We might reason that this assurance makes sense if the hard things we are asked to do are what God wants us to do, but how do we know what God wants us to do? Some practical answers to the question can be found in the experiences of yet another Old Testament hero asked to do hard things—righteous King Hezekiah.

King Hezekiah was, in my estimation, the most worthy king that ever ruled over Judah. Though he was a truly remarkable and righteous man, he had many difficult times. In the year 701 B.C., Hezekiah found his capital city of Jerusalem besieged by a huge Assyrian army. Hezekiah had inherited Assyrian vassalage from his faithless father, King Ahaz, who ignored the counsel of Isaiah and made an alliance with Assyria, thereby voluntarily making Judah a vassal to that brutal and demanding empire (see 2 Kings 16; Isaiah 7).

Each year the king of Assyria exacted a huge tribute from Judah for the privilege of existing. When Hezekiah succeeded his father, he struggled to make the tribute payments. In his fourteenth year, King Hezekiah failed to meet the full payment levied by the Assyrians and they invaded. In desperation, Hezekiah had emptied his treasuries and even cut the gold off the temple doors to try to appease the Assyrians, but to no avail. Hezekiah's failure to meet their full demands was viewed as rebellion. Consequently, Assyria determined to conquer Judah and deport the people, just as they had two decades earlier, to Judah's sister nation of Israel (see 2 Kings 18–19; Isaiah 36–37).

To prepare for the invasion, Hezekiah labored to strengthen the people's obedience to and faith in God. He also worked to fortify the city of Jerusalem, repairing the breaches in the walls and digging his famous water tunnel to bring water into the city so as to be able to withstand a siege (see 2 Kings 18:1–7; Isaiah 22:8–11). When the Assyrians invaded, they swept through much of the nation and eventually surrounded Jerusalem. When the Assyrian military leader Rabshakeh failed to convince Hezekiah and his city to surrender immediately, Sennacherib, the king of Assyria, sent a letter to the besieged Hezekiah warning of utter destruction if he continued to resist. When Hezekiah received the letter he took it to the temple and "spread it before the Lord" (Isaiah 37:14). He then petitioned the Lord for help and direction. The prayer that he offered can teach us much about how to obtain heaven's help when faced with hard things:

> O Lord of hosts, God of Israel, that dwellest between the cherubims, thou art the God, even thou alone, of all the kingdoms of the earth: thou hast made heaven and earth. Incline thine ear, O Lord, and hear; open thine eyes, O Lord, and see: and hear all the words of Sennacherib, which hath sent to reproach the living God. Of a truth, Lord, the kings of Assyria have laid waste all the nations, and their countries, and have cast their gods into the fire: for they were no gods, but the work of men's hands, wood and stone: therefore they have destroyed them. Now therefore, O Lord our God, save us from his hand, that all the kingdoms of the earth may know that thou art the Lord, even thou only. (Isaiah 37:16–20.)

In this humble prayer Hezekiah models several keys to obtaining God's help when faced with great challenges.

1. Hezekiah bears testimony and expresses gratitude to God (see Isaiah 37:16). The king obviously understood that God wants us to confess "his hand in all things" (D&C 59:21) and say our thanks to Him. I believe this is not because God needs to hear our praise and thanks, but rather because as we confess our beliefs and voice our gratitude, our faith, that vital component to accessing the powers of heaven, grows and deepens.

2. Hezekiah carefully explains his challenges to God (see Isaiah 37:17–19). Certainly God is already aware of Hezekiah's situation, but Hezekiah seems to understand that as we take time to detail our dilemmas to God in prayer we start to see things from His perspective. We understand our situation better. We start to see solutions and, most importantly, we invite the spirit of revelation to guide our thoughts and decisions.

3. Hezekiah aligns his will with God's when he pleads, "Save us from his hand, that all the kingdoms of the earth may know that thou art the Lord, even thou only" (Isaiah 37:20). The king understood that prayer is not the act of convincing the Lord to give us what we want, but rather the act of getting ourselves to want what God wants for us. That aligning of wills is a revelatory experience and opens the path for God to enable us to do hard things. It can be an arduous endeavor. Indeed, Enos describes it as a "wrestle . . . before the Lord" (Enos 1:2). The preposition "before" is instructive in Enos's description of prayer. As we seek to pray effectively we do not wrestle "with" God—a wrestling match we would certainly lose, but rather we wrestle before Him. The wrestle seems to be with ourselves as we seek to understand God's will and bring ourselves to adopt and follow it.

The Lord heard Hezekiah's prayer and sent word by Isaiah to assure him of deliverance. The deliverance came in spectacular fashion that night as the angel of the Lord passed through the camp of the besieging Assyrians and destroyed them with a plague (see Isaiah 37:21–38).

I am grateful for the perspective, hope, and assurance the experiences and examples of Moses, Jeremiah, and Hezekiah give us. Our heavenly help in doing hard things may not be as dramatic as that experienced by these great men, but surely as we set aside our fears, make ourselves willing and available to do God's work, faithfully obey His commandments, and pray effectively—expressing our testimony and faith as we pray, carefully explaining to God our challenges, and striving to align our will with God's—He will help us know and do His will. We will understand the promise given by the question the Lord put to Jeremiah, "Behold, I am the Lord, the God of all flesh: is there anything too hard for me?" (Jeremiah 32:27).

NOTE

1. Thomas S. Monson, "You Make A Difference," *Ensign*, May 1988, 41.

Lay Aside the Things of This World, and Seek for the Things of a Better

Sharon Eubank

On January 31, 2008, I got up early in the morning, put on my best church clothes, picked up my fifteen-year-old niece Jordanne, and we drove into Salt Lake City in the predawn hours. President Gordon B. Hinckley had died earlier that week, and people could come and pay their respects at the Conference Center, which his prophetic vision had helped bring about. They opened the building about six a.m. By the time we arrived there was already a line that went around the building. Jordanne and I waited outside in the cold until we could get into the building. As we walked past President Hinckley's casket, she and I were talking a lot about him, including the fact that he was the only prophet that she had known during her lifetime. As we filed past, a phrase came into my mind that I have never forgotten: "I am a friend of the prophets." I thought to myself, Why did my spirit say that? And what does that mean?

I think often about President Gordon B. Hinckley and President Thomas S. Monson and what it means for you and me to live in this time of prophets, seers, and revelators.

Prophets Show Vision

A prophet's sacred role is to lay out the vision of truth—they're seers and they see things as they really are and not as this world sees. We've

---

Sharon Eubank is the director of humanitarian services in the Church Welfare Services department.

heard wonderful sessions during this Women's Conference about what it means to live during a time of prophets. They see the big picture; they see how things that look unrelated actually are interrelated and how we can participate in some of those things.

President Gordon B. Hinckley shared a vision that changes our world as we know it. He said, "Imagine how our own families, let alone the world, would change if we vowed to keep faith with one another, strengthen one another, look for and accentuate the virtues in one another, and speak graciously concerning one another. Imagine the cumulative effect if we treated each other with respect and acceptance, if we willingly provided support. Such interactions practiced on a small scale would surely have a rippling effect throughout our homes and communities and, eventually, society at large."[1]

President Thomas S. Monson said, "Never let a problem to be solved become more important than a person to be loved."[2]

The Prophet Joseph Smith once shared what he called the grand fundamental principle of Mormonism. He said, "I don't care what a man's character is; if he's my friend—a true friend, I will be a friend to him, and [I will] preach the Gospel of salvation to him and give him good counsel. [I will help] him out of his difficulties. Friendship is one of the grand fundamental principles of 'Mormonism.' [It's designed] to revolutionize and civilize the world, and cause wars and contentions to cease and men to become friends and brothers. . . . Friendship is like Brother Turley in his blacksmith shop welding iron to iron; it unites the human family."[3]

Now those just weren't nice words from Joseph. He lived that grand fundamental principle of Mormonism with all of his heart, and people responded to him in a similar way. I recently came across two stories that are so vivid I thought I'd share them with you today.

The first is: "While conversing with his cousin George A. Smith . . . the Prophet wrapped his arms around [George A.] and said [to him] with emotion, 'George A., I love you as I love my own soul!' [And] this left his cousin speechless. In fact, George A. said, 'I could hardly speak, [I was so affected].' In a few [minutes], after regaining his composure, [George A. said back to the Prophet], 'I hope, Brother Joseph, that my whole life and [all my] actions will prove my feelings and the depth of my affection for you.'"[4]

That's the first story.

The second story is about Phineas Young—this is Brigham Young's older brother. He was once in Tiffin, Ohio. And while he was there, he wrote to Willard Richards, who was the Prophet Joseph's secretary, and he said, "I long to see the day when I can again visit my brethren and see the Lord's Prophet, and hear the words of life sweetly distilling from his lips. Give my love to [the Prophet] Joseph when you see him. [And] tell him I'd come to the Rocky Mountains to see him and fight my way through an army of wildcats and Missouri wolves and live on skunks the whole journey."[5] I love that!

To summarize what these powerful modern prophets and Church leaders emphasized:

- We should accentuate the virtues in each other.
- Respect and acceptance have a rippling effect.
- Solving problems is less important than loving people.
- Friendship is designed to revolutionize and civilize the world.
- Wars and contentions should cease.
- Men and women can become friends and family.
- Friendship welds iron to iron. It unites the human family.

If we could condense that into one sentence, it could simply be this: Unity, understanding, and relationships are worth our absolute best efforts.

THE INTERDEPENDENCE OF ALL THINGS

I was taking in my parents' mail while they were on vacation, and so I had all of these stacks—my parents get a ton of catalogs—and as I was taking them into their kitchen, I noticed my dad's *Scientific American*. It was sitting right up on top. I flipped through it and started reading an article about the trillions of tiny bacteria that live inside the human intestinal tract. They operate pretty much as a forest ecosystem does in the natural world. The author was talking about how there are predators in that ecosystem.[6] There are dominant species; there are subordinate species. As I read, I started to get a little queasy because it felt like the African savannah was inside my abdomen.

But this phenomenon shows up from the smallest biology clear up to the largest galaxies. There are different types of systems that interdepend on each other and cooperate together in a unified way so that a cell eventually becomes a human body; a gas bubble can cooperate until it makes a galaxy; and ant colonies are built on the same principle that we build nations on. As I sat in my parents' pink-and-white kitchen it dawned on me: Small things working together in unity to make bigger things is the whole meaning of mortal life. It's why we're here.

We first have the opportunity to unify an intelligence, a spirit, and a body. Those are separate elements, but they've come together in us and they make up our personality. While we're working on that, we get the opportunity to be sealed in a marriage partnership, so that you have a pair of people that grow to understand each other so well that they're unified. They effectively become one in purpose. That sealed pair can be successful and united enough that they create a loyal family circle. In some rare instances, you can extend this unity out to a community or a ward or a group of colleagues. Every once in a while, people can attain that kind of oneness and unity. Enoch did it with a whole city.

This is the whole structure of the universe from the smallest to the biggest. The Lord takes our natural feelings and experiences of friends and He encourages us to extend that out to larger groups. Can you bind together in one a presidency? A ward council? A board? A neighborhood? A ward family? A study group? A teachers quorum? A visiting teacher route? A girls' camp? A prison? What can you do?

I want to tell you a story about a prison. Jim and Karyn Anderson are from Farmington, Utah. He was a bank executive and she was a nurse. They put in their papers to serve a humanitarian mission. They were called to Beirut, Lebanon. It's a stunningly beautiful place that has been scarred by war and factions and disunity and suffering—it's all happened in our lifetime. One day, Elder and Sister Anderson drove way up in the mountains to visit a women's prison. When you get sent to prison in Lebanon, they provide food, but clothing, toiletries, bedding—all of that needs to be supplied by your family. And if you don't have family, then you don't have any of those things. So the Beirut branch of the Church had made some hygiene kits, and the Andersons drove up to the city to deliver them.

When they arrived, they were met by the prison warden. She is a young mother as well as a visionary administrator for that prison. She rolls up her sleeves and works alongside the inmates to make the prison as livable and clean and productive as she can. The Andersons went into one of the cells, and they couldn't help but notice that a woman was lying on one of the mattresses on the floor, sobbing. One of the other inmates took Sister Anderson aside and said to her in English, "Please, help the Chinese."

So Sister Anderson asked, and the warden told them that this woman was from China and she'd been employed by a family in a European country to be their nanny. The family she worked for took a vacation to Lebanon, and brought her along to care for their children. When it was time to depart, they discovered in the airport that they had brought their nanny into the country illegally. She did not have the right visa to enter Lebanon or to leave Lebanon. Instead of dealing with that situation, the family just boarded the airplane and left her there. She was sent to prison to await her trial on immigration violations. In Lebanon that can take up to two years. She had been crying on that mattress for three months. Her family had no idea where she was, and she could not be consoled.

Any kind of real assistance was pretty unlikely. But in this circle of people who knew each other was a friendly inmate who used her skills in English to request some help. There was a sympathetic warden who had a charitable heart, and she asked the Andersons: "Isn't your church good with languages? Can you find a Chinese speaker somewhere who might help us?" There was a member of the Church in the Beirut branch who knew someone at the Chinese embassy. So they placed a phone call, and that person at the embassy called this woman's parents in China. Her parents scraped up the money to buy her a plane ticket, and the Lebanese government allowed her to go back to China.

All of those unlikely people combined together to work on a solution to a single problem. They overcame suspicion, cultural differences, lack of money, lack of communication, and they were successful.

I really believe the people in our own personal circles are mostly a divine gift. There may be a few in there that are thrown in for spice, but I believe that the Lord puts us in proximity on purpose. We can't dismiss the people in our circles.

C. S. Lewis has said something similar that you're perhaps familiar with. He said:

> In friendship . . . we think we have chosen our peers. In reality, a few years' difference in the dates of our births, a few more miles between certain houses, the choice of one university instead of another . . . the accident of a topic being raised or not raised at a first meeting—any of these chances might have kept us apart. But, for a Christian, there are, strictly speaking, no chances. A secret Master of the Ceremonies has been at work. Christ, who said to the disciples, 'Ye have not chosen me, but I have chosen you,' can truly say to every group of Christian friends 'You have not chosen one another but I have chosen you for one another.' The friendship is not a reward for our discrimination and good taste in finding one another out. It is the instrument by which God reveals to each the beauties of all the others.[7]

That's a beautiful quote.

Lay Aside the Things of This World

Interacting with other people in positive, building ways, even if they're using their agency, or their strengths, or their weaknesses, or their perceptions—and we all know this—it's never smooth, it's never easy. Satan delights in using any small thing to break us apart. Breaking up unity is his bread and butter. He does it all day long. Truthfully, we make it pretty easy most of the time.

I really liked that imagery of Phineas Young when he said he would fight through an army of wildcats, and Missouri wolves, and live on skunks the whole time just to make it back to Zion. Because that's about what it takes to lay aside the things of this world. Think for a moment: What do you need to lay aside? What's getting in the way of your peace? What makes up your army of wildcats?—because we all have them.

I'd like to share four things that I have learned from my own bitter experience.

The first thing is to approach situations with humility. You don't know everything that's going on. You aren't the only one that's right. We all have pieces of the truth, but we don't have the whole thing. Only the Lord has the whole thing. So be humble, because your perception could be wrong.

The second thing is to be a builder. Assume that other people have good intent even if you aren't in agreement—they aren't just stupid. They actually want things to work out maybe as much as you do. Jesus was a master at building with the available materials. Satan tears things down. Emphasize what is positive and what you have in common and then see what happens.

The third thing is to practice tolerance and love. Forgive slights. When you can't feel that way, when it feels too hard for you to do, then go to the Father in prayer and ask for some help. Because the power of the Atonement can change the way we feel, and it can change the way we perceive things, and it can change the way we act. That brings unity.

The fourth thing: When something has to change, deal with the person involved directly—and then practice things one, two, and three. The other person's success is really your success.

I'd like to share a couple of examples of these principles. This world operates by the doctrine of Nehor: We prosper by the things that we hoard, by the things that we obtain, that we get, that we buy. Jesus has counterintuitive doctrine to that. He says the things that we secure for our real, permanent life are the things that we absorb, the things that we sacrifice, the things that we lay aside, and the things that we forget.

Most of the time we don't have the power inside ourselves to do those things. We're actually pretty bad at it. But Jesus' Atonement can be the power that we use. He is magnificent at it. He enables us to deflect the hurt and the pain from others and seek a higher purpose. From the Doctrine and Covenants, we see this illustrated:

"Let every [woman] esteem [her] brother [or her sister] as [herself], and practise virtue and holiness before me. And again I say unto you, let every [woman] esteem [her sister as herself]. For what [parent] among you having twelve sons, and is no respecter of them, and they serve him obediently, and he saith unto the one: Be thou clothed in robes and sit thou here; and to the other: Be thou clothed in rags and sit thou there—and looketh upon his sons and saith I am just? Behold, this I have given unto you as a parable, and it is even as I am. I say unto you, be one; and if ye are not one ye are not mine" (D&C 38:24–27).

I often wonder why everything good in this world is so counterintuitive. But it struck me the other day—it's because we don't want to stay in this world. We will eventually pass on to a higher order where different rules apply. The Lord is giving us the opportunity to practice some of those rules right now.

The book *Daughters in My Kingdom* tells about the day when Joseph Smith organized the Relief Society and called Emma Smith to be the first president. He said during that time that his wife's calling fulfilled a prophecy given to him twelve years earlier. Then he sat down with the women there and he read the entire revelation, which is Doctrine and Covenants 25.[8]

In 1830, the Lord gave this beautiful, specific blessing and counsel to Emma Smith. At the end of the revelation the Lord said an interesting thing: "I say unto you that this is my voice unto all" (D&C 25:16). That didn't make very much sense in 1830, but it did in 1842 when the Relief Society was being revealed. At the founding of the Relief Society it became scripture not just for Emma, but for the women of the Church. Those women were being organized to participate in the work of salvation—and not just the twenty women that were in that room when Joseph read it aloud. It was for all of us. What the Lord had said to Emma, He now said to everyone who is a son or daughter in His kingdom: Murmur not. Continue in meekness. Beware of pride. Cleave unto the covenants you have made. Lift up your heart and rejoice (see D&C 25).

In Emma's own words, she said: "I desire the Spirit of God to know and understand myself that I might be able to overcome whatever of tradition or nature that would not tend to my exaltation in the eternal worlds. I desire a fruitful, active mind that I may be able to comprehend the designs of God."[9]

Investments

I have been incredibly blessed in my life to have a friend who is a model of everything that Emma Smith describes. It isn't just that she is nice to me—she is. But she has succored me in my weaknesses, she has borne with me in my troubles, she's rejoiced in good seasons. She has refused to throw my weaknesses in my face. She's inspired me to be a better person. She's talked to me when no one else would. She's told me when I'm making a mistake. And she's given me everyday support and confidence. She's told me ten thousand times that she loves me, she's shared her testimony and her beliefs with me, and prayed with me even when I couldn't. Her friendship is one of the most precious things in my life.

We all do that for our friends; we do those things for each other. But can we also do it for those that we disagree with? Can we exchange enmity for empathy? Because that is a Christlike act, and it's the crux of what I wanted to say today.

Invest in unity, invest in friendship, invest in trust and in forgiveness. Some people will say, "Well, that doesn't pay, because those people always finish last." That may be true—in this world. But we are laying aside the things of this world and we are seeking for things of a better. It isn't all about now. When you know that and when you can do it, then you ally yourselves with a prophetic vision, and you are the friend of the prophet.

Elder Marlin K. Jensen said: "Consider the power of each one of us, 10 million strong [that's how many people were in the Church when he said it], of our own free will and choice reaching out . . . in unconditional friendship. . . . The power is in each one of us to be a friend. Old and young, rich and poor, educated and humble, in every language and country, we all have the capacity to be a friend. . . .

"Having been so richly blessed by Christ's friendship, I pray that we will now be to others what He is to us: a true friend. . . . I know that when we offer ourselves in friendship, we make a most significant contribution to God's work and to the happiness and progress of His children."[10]

Now that's something! If you want to contribute to the progress and happiness of God's children, you can be a friend. You can act in unity. You can forgive.

TESTIMONY

I love Jesus. I can never find the words to say just how I feel. He is the Great Jehovah with the voice of a mighty wind. He is the one and the only true God in a world fraught with opposition and with people who are false imitators of Him. He shows the great power and the good intent of Elohim over all things. He was born on this earth into the most humble of circumstances, and He was the mighty God, but He came as Emmanuel—which means "God with us."[11] He bore the weight of our sins physically and with unsurpassed mental and spiritual courage. He carried our collective load of sin and anguish—and even stupidity. He became our Father because only through Him can we gain life. He has no bureaucracy; He governs everything by love. He seeks reconciliation on every level, from the largest of bringing all mankind who want to come back to Elohim, to the smallest of helping us heal unkind words and selfish acts. His kingdom is made up of smaller things that gather together and cooperate for a larger purpose. He is a royal Son who governs His kingdom with love and temperance and brotherly kindness. He will come a second time to the earth to gather all political kingdoms into one that is His. They will be His people, and they will be of one heart. All knees will bow to Him, not because of His might and power—which are great—but because He brings reconciliation and peace, even to our individual minds and hearts. He is the Prince of Peace.

I testify that the Lord loves each one of us in all of our quirkiness. He listens to us more intently than anybody else in our lives. He never tires of us. He always wants us around Him. We can never give Him too much. He waits with long-suffering to build us, to guide us, to heal us, to tell us the things that we need to know. He is our greatest friend. When we turn around and give those same gifts to others, when we seek to understand others and not to judge them, when we "lay down our weapons of war" and we become the friends of the prophets, then we become the friends of God. This is my prayer for our families, for our relationships, for the councils of the Church, and for every one of us in our hearts.

NOTES

1. Gordon B. Hinckley, *Standing for Something: 10 Neglected Virtues That Will Heal Our Hearts and Homes* (New York: Three Rivers Press, 2000), 57.
2. Thomas S. Monson, "Joy in the Journey," in *Awake, Arise, and Come unto Christ: Talks from the 2008 BYU Women's Conference* (Salt Lake City: Deseret Book 2008), 3.

3. *History of The Church of Jesus Christ of Latter-day Saints*, 7 vols., ed. B. H. Roberts (Salt Lake City: The Church of Jesus Christ of Latter-day Saints, 1932–51), 5:517.
4. *History of the Church*, 5:39.
5. *Journal History of the Church*, 14 December 1842, Church History Library, Salt Lake City, Utah.
6. See B. Brent Finlay, "Stopping Infections: The Art of Bacterial Warfare," *Scientific American*, 15 February 2010; available at http://www.scientificamerican.com/article.cfm?id=the-art-of-bacterial-warfare; accessed 15 October 2012.
7. C.S. Lewis, *The Four Loves* (Orlando: Harcourt Brace, 1988), 89.
8. *Daughters in My Kingdom* (Salt Lake City: The Church of Jesus Christ of Latter-day Saints, 2011), 13.
9. Emma Smith to Joseph Smith, 1844, Church History Library, Salt Lake City.
10. Marlin K. Jensen, "Friendship: A Gospel Principle," *Ensign*, May 1999, 65.
11. See Bible Dictionary, s.v. "Immanuel," 706.

Noble Women: Strength from the Past, Inspiration for the Future

S. Michael Wilcox

Every time I visit Rome, I pay my respects to Marcus. There is an equestrian statue of him made of bronze that graces the top of the Capitoline Hill. There he sits in majestic benevolence overseeing the city as he oversaw the Roman Empire two thousand years ago. He was the last of the five good emperors: a humane, philosophical man who wrote a classic of world literature titled *The Meditations*. He begins by allowing his mind to pass through all the people that had influenced him and lists the qualities and values they instilled in him. They are beautiful tributes offered in praise and gratitude.

I was impressed by Marcus, so I sat down years ago and began to reflect on similar people in my own life. It is an instructive and a humbling experience, and I recommend it. My mind went instinctively, as did his, to family members. Having finished, however, the list seemed somewhat incomplete. I added my heroes and heroines of the scriptures. Then other personalities began to surface in my mind—the nonscriptural breed of men and women. I realized how very, very many past lives had touched

---

S. Michael Wilcox received his PhD from the University of Colorado and recently retired after thirty-seven years as an institute instructor for the Church Educational System. A popular speaker and award-winning author, his previous publications include 10 Great Souls I Want to Meet in Heaven, House of Glory, Fire in the Bones, Sunset, *and* Finding Hope. *He and his late wife, Laurie, are the parents of five children.*

mine, how magnificent humanity is, and how widespread God's involvement has been in the affairs of men.

There are many heroines from the past who have blessed my life. I usually talk about the scriptural ones, but I would like to share a brief story about a woman who has inspired me for decades, who has become particularly dear since the passing of my wife, Laurie. My choice is representative of many others. I hope this woman's life will be an indication of the wide extent of inspiration that may be found outside of scripture or women from Church history.

She was a frail young woman who once loved the sea, and quiet long walks along the shore brought healing. Now she couldn't stand the sight of it. She had been brought to the warmer coast of England for her health, which had been tenuous for years. In light of the present tragedy, she only wanted to return to her house on Wimpole Street. Her family called her "Ba," short for "baby," though she had been christened Elizabeth—Elizabeth Moulton Barrett. The Barrett siblings were a close family of eleven children. Ba's closest, most beloved sibling was Edward, whom she just called "Bro." Now he was dead. The sea had taken him, and she felt it was her fault.

"[And] once *he* held my hand," she recalled years later, "how I remember! and said that he 'loved me better than them all and that he *would not* leave me . . . till I was well,' . . . Ten days from that day, the boat left the shore which never returned; never—and he *had* left me! gone!, and I was grateful to my father for not saying aloud what I said to myself in [my] agony, 'If it had not been for you, he would be alive.'"[1] *If it had not been for you!*

Elizabeth was acquainted with death. Her little sister Mary died when she was eight, then her mother. Sam was next, and then Bro. To love is to place the heart in a vulnerable position, to open it up to pain, and Elizabeth was born with a poet's heart. Love came naturally to her, but the experiences of her earlier life taught her to guard her heart and expect that life at best would only give a small measure of contentment.

"For years together," she wrote, "I lived on the outside of my own life, blindly and darkly from day to day, as completely dead to hope. . . . Nobody quite understood this of me. . . . But God knows what was within."[2]

Deep and abiding happiness was feared. It could so easily turn to suffering. With her own health poor, she huddled over her desk in a private room on Wimpole Street in London, content with composing her poetry, feeling life had offered her all it could. She once wrote, "There is no kind of enjoyment which one can have on this side of the grave without paying its price in pain."[3] Such pessimism for a young woman to feel is touched with an element of pathos and tragedy, yet this she had come to believe. However, Providence had prepared for Elizabeth Barrett its deepest satisfaction and the fulfillment of her highest reaches of passionate yearning. To obtain it, however, would require sacrifice and courage born only in the wellsprings of a loving heart prepared to offer all in order to receive all.

"Once I wished *not* to live,"[4] she said, yet the resiliency of the human soul and its innate desires for happiness, love, and fulfillment—the promise that they will always be possible—was still alive in her heart. In time her very name would be associated with love's highest fulfillments.

She increasingly saw herself as an invalid, confined to the house and her own private room, rarely going out, and eventually needing opium to sleep. This was prescribed for Elizabeth when she was fifteen years old and would haunt her life till the day she died. Social interaction both repelled and frightened her. Her father dominated her. Inactivity had weakened her muscles, and lack of fresh air in her room had further stressed her lungs. She had to be carried down the stairs by her brothers if she wished to be in the sitting room.

She wrote poetry and letters, but few ever invaded the inner sanctum of her private upstairs room. Thus she lived, yet spread through it all was a sense she was missing life's core experiences and that time would not allow her long to discover them. In the language of the time, she was a spinster, approaching her fortieth birthday, and the possibilities of a loving relationship with a man seemed completely out of the equation life had granted her. She had consciously decided "I will never marry." She waited instead for death to take her with the next painful coughing spell.

"It was a lonely life," she wrote. "Books and dreams were what I lived in. . . . And so time passed, and passed."[5] But that was all before a letter arrived and Robert Browning entered her world. It all began with a poem written by Elizabeth, in which she praised Robert's budding creativity.

She was the famous poet, not him. Though she did not expect a response, Robert picked up his pen and wrote to her an amazing letter.

"I love your verses with all my heart, dear Miss Barrett." But there was more. "I do, as I say, love these [verses] with all my heart—and I love you too."[6] They exchanged letters, each realizing they had found another who was sympathetic and understanding. They would write 574 letters in a little less than two years.

Elizabeth believed the exchanges were sufficient in themselves; however, Robert desired to meet her. This threw her into distress, for few ever invaded the privacy of her single-room existence. Here was a man six years her junior who shared her passion for the rhyming line, a man confident in the outside world of society, which she had shunned throughout her life. If they met, would he be disappointed?

She was better on paper. Would face-to-face contact end it all? Finally, she wrote that he could come if he so desired but warned him, "There is nothing to see in me; nor to hear in me."[7] She was only 5' 1" tall, wasted by sickness, slight of frame, thin, dark-complected, with long curled hair and dark brownish-green eyes. What would Robert think of her? "Well!" Elizabeth wrote. "We are friends till Tuesday—and after, perhaps."[8]

Yet in time she would look back on that day and call it, "my great Compensation day."[9] Happiness was courting Elizabeth, had come unbidden into her presence, and she didn't know how to grasp it without Robert's help. But help he would, patiently and selflessly. Robert did not know what to expect as he walked down Wimpole Street, flowers in hand. His image of Elizabeth was of a slight woman, invalid from the cruelty of perpetual illness, permanently disabled with an injured spine. But he was confident.

She awaited him with apprehension on the sofa, still dressed in black since the drowning of Bro. How could he possibly find her pretty? She heard his step on the stair: what would the opening door bring? An hour later she knew joy never expected. Happiness was inviting her forward, urging her to lean into life instead of out of it, and she would not turn away.

Robert asked for another visit and wrote her an unbelievable letter. Would she marry him, and would she do so now?

For two years, they kept their love for each other veiled from others and made their plans. Her health improved under the lifting power of his love and the happiness she felt in his presence. He visited weekly. She walked of her own power down the stairs one day instead of being carried by her brothers, to their shocked and speechless stares. She must get well—so much depended on her now. When she ventured outside on her own power, just short of the one-year mark in their love, she picked a flower and sent it to Robert with the triumphant message: "Look what is inside this letter—look! I gathered it for you today myself when *I* was walking. . . . Are you surprised?"[10]

She wrote a close friend that she was "growing and growing just like the trees—it is miraculous," she said, "the feeling of sprouting life in me and out of me—and now I begin to sleep and to look altogether like another person."[11] She was in love and, perhaps even more important, she was loved. And that changes us. It is one of the deepest discoveries one can make in life—the knowledge that the man you love, or the woman you love, loves you in kind.

He eased her fears that he would in time tire of her: "My own Ba!—My election is made or God made it for me,—and is irrevocable. I am wholly yours. I see you have yet to understand what that implies."[12]

Unknown to Robert, she had written a series of sonnets to him over the course of their letters. One of them simply asked, "If I leave all for thee, wilt thou exchange / And be all to me?"[13] Leaving all would include her father, who would disown her if she married, and the thought frightened her to the point of paralysis. Face-to-face confrontation with him was simply beyond her courage. Secrecy in a private marriage was the only way for them. "Remember that I shall be *killed*," she wrote Robert. "It will be so infinitely worse than you can have an idea."[14] She expressed her worst nightmares: the discoveries of their love and plans by her father.

"I will go for a licence today," Robert responded, "and we can be married on Saturday."[15] "Your words, first and last, have been that you 'would not fail me'—you will not."[16]

Elizabeth responded, "I shall not fail you—I do not, I will not." The die was cast. There would be no bright wedding dresses, bridesmaids, flowers, or celebrations. There would be no announcements, no congratulatory wishes for their happiness, no gifts. There would be only Robert, only Elizabeth—that was more than enough. In a quiet ceremony viewed by only two other people and the priest performing the marriage, Elizabeth Barrett and Robert Browning formed the eternal unit still celebrated as one of the most loving couples in history.

She was *his* Ba now, and that is what he always called her. There was no music, no feasting, and they each returned home after the ceremony, but no woman was happier. "Many, many women who have stood where I stood and to the same end, not one of them of all perhaps, not one, since that building was a church, has had reasons strong as mine, for an absolute trust and devotion towards the man she married,—not one!"[17]

A week later they fled London. She packed light so no one would suspect what she was contemplating. But she had to have his letters, those words of openness.

Robert had always known exactly what he wanted. He wanted Elizabeth. He wanted her with the first letter and first visit. Frail, delicate, dressed in black, vulnerable, awaiting (as her own words affirmed) only "approaching death."[18] Closeted in the dark shadows of her room, he wanted her. He wanted her at the conclusion of almost two years of waiting and dreaming and writing. He never entertained second thoughts. Diminutive, thin, self-assured only in her letters, her poems, and his love—he would always want her. She had to bring those letters—the letters that provide for us today the memorial and inspiration of their togetherness.

She wrote to him on the day they left. "Your letters to me I take with me, let the 'ounces' cry ever so. I *tried* to leave them, and I could not. That is, they would not be left: it was not my fault—I will not be scolded."[19] Then she slipped into the package with her precious letters the sonnets she had written, so beautifully portraying all he meant to her, all he had saved her from, the poems whose existence were yet unknown to Robert, the ink-and-paper testimony of her own love for him—her *Sonnets from the Portuguese.*

Robert took Elizabeth to Italy, where he hoped the warm air and the sunshine and the moderate climate would ease the persistent coughing and her weakened lungs. Her father never forgave her or acknowledged her after the marriage, but her health dramatically improved as they settled in Florence. Everything now thrilled her. "So now ask me again," she wrote to a friend, "if I enjoy my liberty as you expect. My head goes round sometimes, that is all. I never was happy before in my life."[20]

Elizabeth endured four miscarriages, one almost killing her, but gave birth to a robust boy she nicknamed Pen. Robert faced his crucible in the death of his own beloved mother. When nothing she could do would pull him out of his depression, Elizabeth presented him with the forty-four sonnets she had written during their secret courtship. They were deeply personal, and Robert had once remarked in passing that he was not in favor of "putting one's love into verse."[21]

"Do you know," she began tentatively, "I once wrote some sonnets about *you*? There they are, if you care to see them."[22] She was hesitant, nervous.

He read them and fathomed "the depth and breadth and height / My soul can reach" of his wife's love—a love that reached "for the ends of being and ideal Grace." That love rested comfortably in "the level of everyday's / . . . quiet need, by sun and candlelight." It soothed her "old griefs," and fulfilled her "childhood's faith."[23] Everyone should be loved to such a degree. Everyone should love in kind. He had healed her from the anticipation of her own death, hiding in the room at the top of the stairs. Now she pulled him out of the sorrows and pain of his own loss.

Fifteen years they shared life under the sentence of Elizabeth's health, each knowing how it all must end. "You know my cough is always *there*, waiting like a lion in his den,"[24] she wrote, "but I look *over* death,—and upwards."[25]

In the summer of 1861, she complained of a sore throat, which quickly grew into protracted coughing. She had so often rallied that everyone, including Elizabeth, believed she would this time also. She drifted in and out of sleep, but each time she awoke and heard her husband's voice she smiled at him and said she was better. The doctor had increased her morphine for the night, and she stirred a little past three, talking incoherently of a "steamer" which was very "comfortable" and Robert had done "right not to wait."[26] He felt her feet. They were cold even though the room was warm. With the help of their Italian nurse, Robert brought hot water and bathed them. "Well, you do make an exaggerated case of it!" she told him gently, then feeling the effects of the warm water, said, "My hands too."[27]

She seemed to slip into semiconsciousness, which troubled him. Drawing close, he asked her, "Ba, do you know me?" She took him in her arms, smiled, her face peaceful, joyful, and answered, "My Robert—my heavens, my beloved." She kissed him, holding on to him, and kissed him again, and again. "Our lives are held by God," she whispered. He tried to make her more comfortable, but she held him still. "God bless you," she said and repeated it over and over again, "God bless you. God bless you," kissing him continually "with such vehemence." He laid her softly onto the pillow, but she reached her hands to him and kissed the air. Still Robert did not understand she was dying. "Are you comfortable?" he asked. "Beautiful," she answered.

It was her last word. He took her into his arms again, supporting her head. She tried to cough, but the struggle was faint. Her face contracted a tiny bit, then all was silent. It was the nurse, Annunziata, who finally said, "*Quest' anima benedetta è passata!*" ("This blessed spirit has passed.")[28]

She passed happy, smiling, in the arms of the man to whom she had given her soul so many brief years ago when she read the words contained in his first letter, "I love your verses with all my heart, dear Miss Barrett. . . . And I love you too."

"She is with God," Robert wrote to his sister, "who takes from me the life of my life. . . . I shall live out the remainder [of my life] in her direct influence, endeavouring to complete mine . . . imperfect now, but so as to take the good she was meant to give me. . . . I shall now go and sit with herself—my Ba, for ever."[29]

Their love was *beautiful,* and it was rare. It was a love sanctified in gratitude in that neither one of them expected to know it. But experience it they did in a manner that is so beautiful, so exceptional, as Elizabeth knew when she drew her last breath—as Robert knew when he wept with a close friend and simply cried, "I want her, I want her!"[30]

Elizabeth was buried in an English cemetery in Florence where her grave can still be visited today, and Robert returned to England with their son. He never remarried but went on to write some of his most powerful poetry—as Elizabeth believed he could and willed that he would. Yet the gift they gave to the world was not contained in rhymed meters or beautiful imagery. It is in the love that ran pure as sunlight between them. It is in the hope of fulfillment and joyful giving that their lives seem to promise us all if we can learn the sharing of the heart as they did.

We never know what life will bring us with the next ticking of the clock—the death of a most beloved brother in a squall at sea or the sound of a loving man's eager footsteps echoing on the stairs, climbing up to us. What Elizabeth has taught me is never to doubt the possibilities of the footsteps on the stairs. Life is, at heart, simply "beautiful,"[31] as she said. She once testified, "Dancing is better for the soul than fasting,"[32] and cheerfulness is a Christian duty, the proof of a higher spiritual life than melancholy. I have a lovely friend who coined the expression, "the unexpected life"—a life she is living, as am I since the death of my wife, Laurie. Neither one of us received what we anticipated. I think the first time I heard it, I assumed immediately that a life that is "unexpected" was by definition the undesired one—the dreams unfulfilled, the anticipated joys fading with the passing years. But Robert and Elizabeth's love cries out against that perception. The unexpected life can be filled with promise, of answers beyond our dreams, and we must never stop believing this. Around the corner may be an upset boat and a missing brother, but it may also be the beginning of 574 letters filled with hopes and dreams long since abandoned.

Elizabeth Barrett Browning felt she was born for some eternal good. "I always imagine that I was sent on earth for some purpose," she wrote. "I know, I understand not how this is but I feel it to my heart's core and so strong is this feeling that it amounts almost to presentiment!"[33]

She joined with Robert in presenting to us love at its highest level and that oh-so-important hope we must never let die within us, so that happiness, however far or impossible it seems to be, may yet come climbing up the stairs into our lives.

Elizabeth wrote that people need "educating into gladness."[34] Joy, happiness, laughter, optimism are not always inherent in our personalities or circumstances of mortality. We are certainly born to these things as part of our inheritance from God, who wishes our joy. But they also need to be educated into us. It is especially tragic when they are educated out of us, as they were early in Elizabeth's life. "Nothing is more true to me," she said, "than that *gloom* is an immoral thing."[35] She wrote that to her sister just before she died. "And as for solitude," she continued, "I *know* it to be full of temptation."[36]

It is not sufficient that we simply wait for gladness in beyond-the-veil compensations as she once did, fearful of feeling happiness lest it be taken from us. Here and now the possibilities reach out to us. The unexpected life may be the best life we can imagine, not the shattered one. Just before her quiet marriage, Elizabeth hinted to a friend what it all meant to her. "God intended me compensation even in the world and that the latter time would be better for me than the beginning."[37]

The human ear must ever be tuned for happiness climbing the stairs toward us. Both Robert and Elizabeth knew they were blessed in each other and could appreciate and feel gratitude and happiness at the deepest levels. "I, who by long sorrowfulness and solitude, had sunk into the very ashes of self-humiliation. Think how I must have felt to have listened to [words of love] from such a man. A man of genius and miraculous attainments . . . but of a heart and spirit beyond them all!"[38]

My wife, Laurie, introduced me to Elizabeth Barrett Browning. Laurie's grandparents gave her on her high school graduation Elizabeth's *Sonnets from the Portuguese*. Since she showed them to me after our marriage, the Brownings became a part of our own relationship. When she was dying, I whispered their words into her ear, and the last thing I did before veiling her face was to repeat to her one of Elizabeth's sonnets. I too know what it means to cry out, "I want her!" Yet Elizabeth would undoubtedly respond to me, "All our grief is foolish, if we could see aright."

Personally, I must not, as Elizabeth once counseled a friend who was grieving, "disturb her where she is, by unreasonable sadness,—but rather by faith and assurance draw her 'nearer and nearer.' And still nearer till the re-union forever."[39] Beautiful words—the words of a poet. It is difficult at such moments to know what to say, the feelings run so deep, the sorrow in our hearts, certainly in mine, so inexpressible. But Elizabeth rescued me and placed hope in my soul and words in my mouth—the words of love I believe Laurie heard and accepted and understood and sent back again. Eve testified that it was necessary for us to pass through sorrow that we may know what true joy is.

Perhaps the greatest knowledge we gain as we "pass through" is the assurance of how precious it is to have someone to love, as Robert loved

Elizabeth and Elizabeth loved Robert. To gain that understanding at the level of eternal enduring is worth the grieving and the deep poignancy of those last moments in Salt Lake, or in Florence, as I am sure the Brownings would affirm. And there is always the hope Elizabeth so wondrously expressed in the second to the last of her beautiful *Sonnets from the Portuguese,* the one I whispered to my Laurie at our last parting: "I love thee with the breath, / Smiles, tears, of all my life!—and, if God choose, I shall but love / Thee better after death."[40]

May Elizabeth lift you to higher levels of life's fulfilling, as she has lifted me, and lift others as long as the soul can hope, as long as the soul can love, is my sincere prayer.

NOTES

1. Julia Markus, *Dared and Done: The Marriage of Elizabeth Barrett and Robert Browning* (London: Bloomsbury, 1995), 23.
2. Ibid., 83.
3. In Margaret Forster, *Elizabeth Barrett Browning: A Biography* (New York: Doubleday, 1988), 51.
4. Ibid., 103.
5. Markus, *Dared and Done,* 28.
6. Ibid., 3.
7. Forster, *Elizabeth Barrett Browning,* 147.
8. Ibid., 148.
9. Markus, *Dared and Done,* 38.
10. Ibid., 49; emphasis added.
11. Ibid., 50.
12. Ibid., 44.
13. Elizabeth Barrett Browning, *Sonnets from the Portuguese* (Portland, ME: Thomas B. Mosher, 1910), "Sonnet 35," 37.
14. Markus, *Dared and Done,* 72.
15. Forster, *Elizabeth Barrett Browning,* 178.
16. Ibid., 178.
17. Ibid., 180.
18. *Juvenilia,* "The Battle of Marathon," Book IV, lines 319–20.
19. Markus, *Dared and Done,* 74.
20. Ibid., 88.
21. Ibid., 164.
22. Forster, *Elizabeth Barrett Browning,* 237.

23. *Sonnets from the Portugese,* "Sonnet 43," 45.
24. *The Letters of Elizabeth Barrett Browning to Her Sister Arabella,* vol. 2, ed. Scott Lewis (Winfield, KS: Wedgestone Press, 2002), 122.
25. Markus, *Dared and Done,* 211, 190.
26. Robert Browning's letter to his sister Sarianna, 30 June 1861, reproduced in *Robert and Elizabeth Barrett Browning: Everyman's Library Pocket Poets* (New York: Alfred A. Knopf, 2003), 247.
27. Ibid., 248.
28. Ibid.
29. Ibid., 248–49.
30. Mrs. Sutherland Orr, *The Life and Letters of Robert Browning, Volume 2* (Boston: Houghton Mifflin, 1895), 358.
31. Ibid., 248.
32. Markus, *Dared and Done,* 314, 308.
33. Ibid., 133.
34. Forster, *Elizabeth Barrett Browning,* 213.
35. Markus, *Dared and Done,* 314.
36. Ibid., 314.
37. Forster, *Elizabeth Barrett Browning,* 173.
38. Markus, *Dared and Done,* 83.
39. Ibid., 310, 308.
40. *Sonnets from the Portuguese,* "Sonnet 43," 45.

The Vital Role of Women in the Gospel

Linda K. Burton, Relief Society general president; Carole M. Stephens, first counselor; Linda S. Reeves, second counselor

Sister Burton: Welcome! I'm Linda Burton, this is my first counselor, Carole Stephens, and my second counselor, Linda Reeves. We're delighted to be here.

We're hoping that as you leave this Women's Conference, and maybe even as you leave this session, you'll leave with something specific that the Holy Ghost will teach you. We hope you'll see patterns that will help you throughout this conference. It's interesting how the Holy Ghost weaves things together to teach us things we need to do. We're hoping

---

Linda K. Burton is the Relief Society general president. She has served in various callings in every Church auxiliary. She and her husband, Craig P. Burton, are the parents of six children and have nineteen grandchildren.

Carole M. Stephens is the first counselor in the Relief Society general presidency. She has also served on the Relief Society general board; in various auxiliary callings; as a Church service missionary; and as a seminary teacher. She studied early childhood education at Weber State University in Ogden, Utah. She and her husband, Martin R. Stephens, are the parents of six children and have seventeen grandchildren.

Linda S. Reeves is the second counselor in the Relief Society general presidency. She served with her husband when he presided over the California Riverside Mission, and as a stake Relief Society president, ward Relief Society first counselor, Young Women president, young single adult adviser, Sunday School teacher, and Primary chorister. She graduated from Brigham Young University with a bachelor's degree in special education. She and her husband, Melvyn K. Reeves, are the parents of thirteen children.

that you go home with an increased desire to be better disciples of Jesus Christ and that you'll understand that you have a vital role to play as women in the gospel.

In the years to come, we look forward to getting to know each of you, but in this setting, we'll simply introduce ourselves. We've decided to do this collectively rather than individually. So here are a few facts about us. Collectively we've been married 113 years. Between us we have twenty-five children—fifteen daughters and ten sons. We have sixty-three grandchildren—thirty-four granddaughters and twenty-nine grandsons—you can see we're tilting toward Relief Society, can't you?

Sister Stephens: Collectively we have lived in or visited sixty-six countries on six continents. We have served in Relief Society for a total of forty-three years. And we have served as visiting teachers—are you ready for this?—for 115 years.

Sister Reeves: We have served in Young Women for twenty years, in Primary for twenty-three years, and, again collectively, in other Church callings including Sunday School for thirty-three years. And interestingly enough, each of us has had an opportunity not only to serve in parent-teacher associations for many years, but we've all been politically active.

Sister Stephens: Collectively, we've had many mortal experiences, either in our immediate families or in our extended families. Those have included unemployment, cancer, drug addiction, miscarriages, infertility, twins, death, divorce, adoptions, disability, financial loss, depression, alcoholism, and pornography. These experiences have strengthened our testimonies, and have created opportunities for us to rely on and to be strengthened through the atoning power of our Savior, Jesus Christ.

Sister Reeves: Sister Zina Young, a former general Relief Society president, said, "Sisters, it is for us to be wide awake to our duties."[1] So today we're going to talk a little bit about what we need to do to recognize our duties and to be wide awake to those.

Sister Burton: Being wide awake comes in knowing that we all have a vital role to play in Heavenly Father's kingdom. We may be in different circumstances. Some of us are married, some of us are not; some of us are divorced, some of us are widowed. But we all have two things in common that we know for sure, and we can read this in Doctrine and

Covenants 138. I'll just briefly paraphrase it. We know we received our first lessons in the world of spirits and we know were prepared to come forth in this time to labor in His vineyard to do His work. As we discuss the vital work we were sent here to do, we're going to try and pretend like we're sitting around a kitchen table and that you're peeking in our window so we won't be so nervous.

Sister Stephens: The Lord defines His work in Moses 1:39—you all probably know this and could repeat it with me: "For behold, this is my work and my glory, to bring to pass the immortality and eternal life of man." When the Prophet Joseph restored Relief Society, he said this: "The [Relief Society] is not only to relieve the poor, but to save souls."[2] It is vital that each of us understand our responsibility and our duties. It's vital that we understand our work, be prepared to participate, and take our place in God's work. His work is called a work of salvation. In the Church sometimes we use big broad terms like "a work of salvation," and as soon as we say that, you think, *That is too hard. That is too big. I can't do that.* But we hope to show you today that the work of salvation is really quite easy, and it's something that we do every single day.

Sister Reeves: Linda, I wonder if you would mind sharing with us the story about the fly.

Sister Burton: As we talk about the vital role we have as women, the first thing we want to remember is that everything we do in the Church is to help us increase our faith in our Heavenly Father, and increase our personal righteousness. Our Relief Society purposes are the work of our Heavenly Father. I was in church one day and a darling sister whom I love came up to me and said, "I would just love to be a fly on the wall and see what goes on behind closed doors in your house." Frankly, it startled me, because I thought, what am I doing in church that she thinks may be different in my house? It was a good wake-up call for me to think, *Am I living the gospel in my home as well as I appear to be living it at Church?* Sister Reeves, what about your mirror story?

Sister Reeves: Well, I had a similar experience. I was fortunate to inherit my grandmother's mirror, a mirror that she had hung in the entryway of her home. I put it in our entryway after she passed away. One day I was passing that mirror and looked at my face. I'd just been with my husband and children in the other room, and I thought, *My face is so sour.* I thought, *Is that the face that my children and husband are seeing all day long in our home?* So that mirror has become a sweet reminder of paying attention to what expression is on my face, which, of course, is reflective of what's going on inside me.

Sister Stephens: Linda, I think you also shared with us a story about how you decided to change when you saw that look on your face in the mirror.

Sister Reeves: Many years ago now, when I had just four young children—in fact, our oldest was not quite five (I had always looked forward to motherhood and loved those little children)—I was overwhelmed. My house was almost always a mess, and often the children were not dressed until noon. If they had been fed at all, it was because they'd gone on into the kitchen and gotten themselves cold cereal. But I realized I was not enjoying motherhood, mainly because I didn't like the mother that I was. I was having a hard time maintaining control, being happy, and accomplishing all that I felt like I needed to do. I found myself with a desperate feeling. I wasn't alone in this—my husband was feeling the same way. We were both overwhelmed. So we determined that we would spend some time over the next little while in fervent prayer to our Heavenly Father and that our scripture study would be with the end in mind of finding out what the Lord would have us do so that we could get things under control. We went to the temple and we pled with the Lord over a period of months. And the answer that came was really so simple, and something that we hear all the time. In fact, I've been so touched by those that have spoken today, seeing that the revelation that comes from our Heavenly Father, what our prophets, seers, and revelators have told us, is truly the same for all of us. What came to me and to my husband was that every day we needed to have our personal prayers and prayer with our children. Every day, we needed to read the scriptures individually and also with our children. Each Monday night—you know the answer to that one—family home evening. We should also try to get to the temple as often as we could, even with those four little children.

Now does this mean that nothing else was important? Certainly there are other important things—service is very important. But the Lord was telling us to prioritize, to concentrate on those four things. Do those all-important things every day, and everything else that's important will fall into place. I've even had women who knew me well, who said years later, "Oh, Linda, I remember coming to your home and ringing the doorbell and one of the children would come in the door, and if they had any clothes on at all it was just underwear." When they've told me that, the thought would come into my mind, *Yes, but did you know that we had prayer and read scriptures that day?* And you know, when I say that things haven't been easy, believe me, they haven't. It's been a hard road, and we've had some good adversity. But the confidence before the Lord, and the sweetness that has come into our lives as I've seen our children come to know the Savior, to really know who He is, and to know of His Atonement, because we tried to read the scriptures, and we were praying, as I look over and watch them and see that they're trying to do the same things that we did, there is so much peace and happiness in my life.

Sister Burton: You heard those vital things that needed to happen. Those are the things that count.

Sister Stephens: Thanks for sharing that with us. I think every one of us in this room has had that same moment in our lives when we had that awakening, that change of heart when the Spirit was speaking to us and telling us that something needed to change. Then, when we take a step back and refocus a little bit, we realize that what we had stepped away from were the most essential things. I had a little granddaughter who taught me a very important lesson about staying focused on the Savior. We had some grandchildren visiting from Arizona, and our little granddaughter Mailee and her brothers were helping me to set up some decorations for Christmas. I had set up previously a little nativity, and I noticed as we were doing some other things that Mailee went over and was rearranging it. My first thought was, *I'll just fix it when she leaves.* So I let her play with it, and after she left, and I finished up with the Christmas decorations, I went back into the family room and thought, *Oh, I should fix that nativity*. I walked over and looked down at the nativity and I didn't need to fix it at all. I just started to cry as I looked down and saw that little Mailee had put the manger in the center, and she had all the little animals tucked in tight around that manger, and they were peeking in. Then she had all of the people in a circle around the animals. And everybody was focused on the center. They were all facing the Savior. I have that little nativity in my office, arranged the same way, and I look at it often—it reminds me where my focus needs to be in everything that I do.

In Matthew 14, we also learn a great lesson from Peter about focus. You know the story—the Savior came and was walking on the water, and the disciples looked out and they were afraid. They thought it was a spirit. The Savior said to them, "Be of good cheer; it is I. Be not afraid. And Peter answered . . . and said, Lord, if it be thou, bid me come unto thee on the water. And he said, Come" (Matthew 14:27–28). So Peter did. He got out of the boat, and he started to walk toward the Savior, and he was walking on the water. But then he lost his focus, didn't he? He took his eyes off the Savior, because it says "when he saw the wind boisterous, he was afraid" (Matthew 14:30). So the winds and the waves were coming up around him and he saw them instead of the Savior. He lost his focus. When he saw that, and became afraid—he was filled with fear—it says he was beginning to sink. That's one of my favorite words in this account—"beginning" to sink. He was not sunk yet (see Matthew 14:27–30). All of us at some point in our lives are beginning to sink. Every day of our lives we might be sinking a little bit. And some days we might feel like we're just a nose above water. But we are never sunk if we bring our focus back to center; the center of our lives is our Savior, Jesus Christ.

We also learn a great lesson in John 4 about the woman at the well—that's what we've come to know her as. This is such a wonderful story with so many layers, and so many teachings. But for today, we'll talk about the ways that we can liken her to ourselves. First of all, we know that this woman was less than perfect. Linda, I think you wanted to share something about that part.

Sister Reeves: I would. Isn't it amazing, when you think about the fact that the Savior, who was worn out, went to this particular well, among the Samaritans, and Heavenly Father guided Him to this woman, who had made some mistakes in her life. Many mistakes. And yet because of Heavenly Father's love, He sent the Savior, all by Himself, to this particular woman, to offer her living water.

Sister Stephens: We read in the scriptures that the Savior started to teach her, and she didn't understand at first. Sometimes when we open the scriptures, we have a hard time understanding them too. But the Savior didn't give up on her. He continued to teach. That's another lesson for us. Don't give up on the scriptures. If you immerse yourself in the scriptures, pretty soon they'll start to talk to you. So don't give up on yourself; keep trying. Secondly, He did not judge her. He knew who she was. He questioned her about her life. He knew that she had had five husbands, and the man that she was with now was not her husband. He knew all of that but He did not judge her. He continued to teach her, and it worked. She felt His love, and she started to understand what He was trying to say to her. When she had the faith to ask Him, He filled her with living water, the living water that only He can give. Then, when she was filled, she exercised her faith, and she went out and shared with others (see John 4:28–29). Sometimes we get to the part where she's received the living water and that's the end of the story. But if you read further, the Savior's talking about "the [field is] white already to harvest" (John 4:35), and the woman has gone before Him. She has gone into the city to testify, and to share this living water with others. She says to them, come and see: "Come, see a man" (John 4:29). As she planted these seeds, she prepared the ground so that when the Savior and His disciples came later, they were able to teach. In verse 42 it says, "And [they] said unto the woman, Now we believe, not because of thy saying: for we have heard him ourselves, and know that this is indeed the Christ, the Saviour of the world."

To many people this woman was insignificant. In the first verse, it says she even asks Him: Why are you asking me, a Samaritan, for a drink of water? You know that the Jews have nothing to do with Samaritans. And when the disciples came back they questioned as well—they marveled that He even talked to her.

To some she may have seemed insignificant, but not to the Savior. He knew her. He knew her potential, and He needed her to participate in His work, and He filled her with that living water, knowing that when she was filled, she would go out and share with others.

Sister Burton: I think there's an interesting little footnote to this story. In verse 28 we read that the woman left her water pot and went to testify. She thought she had come just to get water. But what she left with was so much more—it was really the vital, living water that she left with that enabled her to go out and serve. How do we get that? What's the how of that? It sounds great, but what do we do to get that living water?

Sister Belle Spafford, one of our wonderful Relief Society general presidents, gave this suggestion. She said, "The average woman today, I believe, would do well to appraise her interests, evaluate the activities in which she is engaged, and then take steps to simplify her life, putting things of first importance first, placing emphasis where the rewards will be [the] greatest, and [the] most enduring, and ridding herself of the less rewarding activities."[3] That's the how.

Sister Reeves: When I think about the woman leaving the water vessel behind, it makes me think that when we turn toward the Savior and follow Him, we must leave the world behind, and those things that are unimportant.

Sister Stephens: We know that one of our purposes in Relief Society is to strengthen families and homes. When we as mothers and grandmothers and sisters and aunts and daughters are focused on the Savior, we can share and strengthen our children and grandchildren.

Sister Burton: That's one of the most vital things that we do.

Sister Stephens: Absolutely. It makes us more intentional parents when we keep eternal life in perspective, when we keep the Lord's work in focus—"for this is my work and my glory" (Moses 1:39)—when we're focused on that, it makes us more intentional. Our daughter Melanie texted us a picture of our little granddaughter Halle right after general conference on Sunday, 1 April 2012. Halle is six years old, and she was watching general conference with a notebook and a pencil. She was coloring or drawing pictures and writing down the things that she learned from listening to general conference. Now I would guess that a six-year-old Halle did not come up with the idea to have a tablet and a pencil, and to be watching conference and drawing pictures and making notes about the speakers. Halle gets it because her mother gets it. Because Melanie is keeping her vessel filled, she is able to bless her family. Melanie is teaching Halle vital things, and you can see that Halle got it. She was talking about temporal and spiritual needs. And then she wrote on her tablet, "We are strong grils." Don't you love that? She's six years old and she knows she is a "strong gril" with a purpose.

Sister Burton: It's all about intentional parenting, isn't it? What's one way we can do that? Linda, how can we help?

Sister Reeves: Well, I'm reminded of a few years ago when now-Bishop Gary E. Stevenson of the Presiding Bishopric told or suggested to us in general conference that we take a virtual tour of our homes. You probably remember that. He suggested that we close our eyes and imagine going in through the front door. What do we see on our walls? What magazines and books are there? Is there a place in the home that's set aside for scripture study, where maybe the scriptures are in a bookcase, readily accessible for us to use? What kind of feeling is there in the home? What kind of conversations go on? Is there contention? It reminds me that later in his talk, he told us to say the word *temple*. "Temple." And then "holy temple." "Home." "Holy home."[4] That is what we're trying to create, isn't it? A place that is a refuge from the storm for our families, for our parents, our brothers and sisters, friends—whoever comes there. I had an experience when we moved to Utah about fifteen years ago and my children were beginning to get to know children at school. My twins were invited over to play to one of the homes, and I didn't know this mother at all. The twins were very insistent; they wanted to go. So I thought, *Well, I'll just take them over there and I'll go into the home and meet this mother.* As soon as the mother opened the door, right there in the entryway was a beautiful painting of the Savior. I could feel the feeling in that home immediately and felt great about those girls going in.

Sister Burton: That's intentional parenting again, isn't it? We can compare this principle of being intentional with the story of Lehonti. If we are not in tune with the Spirit and intentional in our parenting, we can come down by degrees if we're not careful. I remember Sister Elaine Dalton talking about that. She said, "Could it be that . . . we tolerate, then accept, [then] embrace the vice that surrounds us?"[5] We have to be so careful. We have to see where the chinks in our armor are. I loved Sister Ruth Todd's example in this conference of going shopping with her daughters.[6] She was like a warrior. She did not come down—unlike Lehonti, who did come down, by degrees. It's interesting as you look at the story of Lehonti in Alma 47. There are a couple of phrases that show the process of his "coming down." At first it says he "durst not" (Alma 47:11)—in other words, he didn't dare come down. Then it said he "would not." And then Amalickiah could not get him to come down until he says, "Okay, you can bring your guards with you" (see Alma

47:12–13). Sometimes we feel a little more secure if our friends come with us, then we can more easily "come down." But it works the other way too—I think as Relief Society sisters, if we're holding on together and bracing each other up, we can stay on the strait and narrow path together and make a positive difference for good in each others' lives.

I'm thinking of a wonderful mother who saw some concerns in her home with her oldest daughter, who was just starting junior high. She could see her beginning to "come down." When she investigated, she found that this girl was associating with some friends who were bringing her down, ridiculing her standards. This was a wise mom, a guardian of her home. She was taking a "virtual tour," just as Sister Reeves talked about earlier. She decided that she'd better pray. Because her spiritual vessel was full of living water, when she prayed, the answer that came to her was "Take her to the temple." So she arranged to start taking this daughter every Friday morning to the temple. Soon they branched out and started inviting other mothers and their daughters in their ward to go with them to the temple. You can imagine what the result of this story is—the daughter was strengthened, the mother was strengthened, and friendships were formed with girls who did not bring her down. But it all began with a virtual tour and intentional parenting, to strengthen a daughter, a home, and a family. That's that's the vital role we as women play in the gospel.

Sister Reeves: I love that she was so prayerful in asking Heavenly Father to guide and direct her with the very specific thing that would help her daughter.

Sister Burton: Isn't it interesting that this keeps going back to the temple and prayer and scriptures and so on? It's not always a mother that wields the influence for good. Sometimes it's a friend—and I will tell this story. This is my story. At age thirteen I was struggling a little bit, and Heavenly Father brought a young single adult woman into my life. She was serving as a missionary at the time. She happened to see that this little thirteen-year-old girl was insecure and needed some shoring up. I remember kneeling with her in prayer, and her praying for me. That was something I will never forget—it was life-changing for me. I knew that she loved me and I knew she knew her Heavenly Father. She wielded great influence on my life at a critical time and I am thankful forever for her.

Sister Reeves: Do you mind if I share a quote from President Boyd K. Packer? There is such a great promise that he gave. He said, "I say again that [we] today are . . . in enemy territory with a declining standard of morality. . . . As a servant of the Lord, I promise you that you will be protected and shielded from the attacks of the adversary if you will heed the promptings that come from the Holy Spirit. Dress modestly; talk reverently; listen to uplifting music. Avoid all immorality and personally degrading practices. Take hold of your life and order yourself to be valiant."[7] Don't you love that? Order yourself to be valiant. We can do it.

Sister Burton: That reminds me of the scripture in 2 Nephi 25:26. There's no more intentional parenting than this, and nothing that will strengthen your home more. You'll remember this scripture: "And we talk of Christ, we rejoice in Christ, we preach of Christ, we prophesy of Christ, and we write according to our prophecies, that our children may know to what source they may look for a remission of their sins," which, of course, is the Atonement of our Savior Jesus Christ. Can I tell one more story?

Sister Reeves: Please—we love stories!

Sister Burton: This is one last intentional parenting story. I saw this happen just a few years ago in a land far away. I saw a little ten-year-old girl stand up in fast and testimony meeting, and she said, "My mom and my dad had this crazy idea to send us to these local schools, and we don't even know the language. It's been really kind of hard." She continued, "But my mom has helped us memorize some scriptures each day in our family devotional. It sure helps me when times are getting tough." She went on to say, "In fact, my favorite one comes from 2 Timothy 1:7." And she rattled it off: "For God hath not given us the spirit of fear; but of power, and of love, and of a sound mind." What a great example of intentional parenting and the importance of strengthening a home. Her mother was filling her vital role in the lives of her family.

Sister Reeves: I would love to relate Alma's experience. Alma the Elder had learned all that he knew about the gospel from Abinadi, and then he was able to gather many of the people out with him—they had to hide out. We read the beautiful story about the people gathered at the Waters of Mormon (see Mosiah 18), where Alma talks about bearing one another's burdens and mourning and comforting one another—that these are the covenants that we make at the time of baptism. How beautiful and important those covenants are. Let me mention maybe a verse or two: "And it came to pass that he said unto them: Behold, here are the waters of Mormon (for thus were they called) and now, as ye are desirous to come into the fold of God, and to be called his people [*His* people], and are willing to bear one another's burdens, that they may be light; yea, and are willing to mourn with those that mourn; yea, and comfort those that stand in need of comfort, and to stand as witnesses of God . . . in all places that ye may be in, even until death" (Mosiah 18:8–9)—what incredible covenants we make to take care of one another!

Sister Burton: That's right.

Sister Reeves: I know you mentioned once how much you love the feeling you get about what they did.

Sister Burton: Covenants are what sustain us—that's our armor we've talked about, but what I love is the verse that comes after the one you've just shared. It says, "And now when the people had heard these words, they clapped their hands for joy, and exclaimed: This is the desire of our hearts" (Mosiah 18:11).

Sometimes I think we allow our covenants to drag us down. But they should make us joyful. We need to cleave to those covenants with joy in our hearts. I love that they clapped their hands for joy for those covenants.

Sister Reeves: After reading about them remembering their covenants, I love turning to the next page and reading verse 21, "And he commanded them that there should be no contention one with another, but that they should look forward with one eye, having one faith and one baptism, having their hearts knit together in unity and in love one towards another" (Mosiah 18:21).

As we continue to read, we find that they gave, in verse 28, "their substance of their own free will and good desires toward God, and to those priests that stood in need, yea, and to every needy, naked soul." Isn't it interesting that they mention priests there? Sometimes I don't ever think about the bishop or the stake president having needs. We expect or think that they're serving us.

Sister Burton: That's right. It goes back to the story of the woman at the well. Unless our vessels are full, we can't share that water with someone else. We've got to have that vital water inside us to be able to do that.

Sister Stephens: These things that we've discussed, they're all things that come naturally to us. Joseph Smith said, "You are now placed in a situation where you can act according to those sympathies which God has planted in your bosoms. If you live up to these principles, how great and glorious!"[8]

Being spiritually prepared allows us to be willing and able and worthy vessels for the Lord to use to take care of these things that need to be taken care of every single day. Elder M. Russell Ballard calls them "small but deliberate deeds"[9]—I love that. They're deliberate because we're praying and asking, "What can I do?" Heavenly Father, if He knows that we're willing and worthy, will use us.

In 3 Nephi 17, beginning in verse 7, Jesus Christ says, "Have ye any that are sick among you? Bring them hither. Have ye any that are lame, or blind, or halt, or maimed, or leprous, or that are withered, or that are deaf, or that are afflicted in any manner? Bring them hither and I will heal them." He needs us. He needs us to bring them to Him.

We talked about the work of salvation earlier. The work of salvation is temporal. The work of salvation is also spiritual. But we don't need an official mission call to go out and serve and "bring them" to Him. Those who are in need are right next door. They are right across the street. They are right around the corner. He knows who they are. Sometimes we say they're "lost." Well, they're not lost to Him. He knows right where they are, and He will use us to go out and bring them to Him if we are willing and if we are prepared.

Sister Burton: Elder M. Russell Ballard has said, "Every sister in this Church who has made covenants with the Lord has a divine mandate to help save souls, to lead the women of the world, to strengthen the homes of Zion, and to build the kingdom of God."[10] We have a divine mandate to do that. Sister Reeves, you have a story to share about visiting teaching that will illustrate this really well.

Sister Reeves: I would love to share that. Someone shared this letter with me recently. It was written to a former missionary who's been home for thirty years and received this letter not long ago.

"Dear Elder [Jensen], a very loving greeting from our area of the world. I hope you remember who I am and also remember my husband and children. Thirty years ago you taught the gospel to us. We were active in the Church for several years, but then because of too much pride, we stopped going to church twenty-five years ago. About nine months ago I received a call from a sister who said she had just moved into our ward, and that I didn't know her but that she was my new visiting teacher and wanted to come visit me. I told her I did not go to that church anymore. She said that was okay, she still wanted to come over and visit me and get to know me anyway. Well, she came over, and I remember that first visit. I asked her—she looked so young—I asked her how old she was, and she was twenty-four. I thought, how can a twenty-four-year-old teach me anything? She was very kind and bore a strong testimony about the Book of Mormon. I thought that she would visit me just this once, but I was wrong. It was the first of many visits. She bore a very strong testimony that Jesus loved me and that I was needed in the ward. Nearly six weeks ago, my mother died. The first person to arrive at my home was my visiting teacher. She spent the day with me. She asked me if I had a Book of Mormon that she could use. Then she read to me some very comforting scriptures about the plan of salvation and gave her testimony that I would see my mother again. The Spirit was very strong. I felt that the Lord loved me because my visiting teacher loves me. I want you to know that we are going to church again. I want to thank you for being a missionary. And I am so grateful for this young, twenty-four-year-old woman, who I didn't think knew anything, who has touched my heart. Our three children are now grown, and we hope that they will return to the Church as well, for we are preparing to go to the temple. With much love, [this sister]."[11]

Sister Stephens: Right next door. Right around the corner. Yes, we do it every day.

Sister Stephens: We bring them—it's a natural thing for us.

Sister Burton: We bring them so that they can be healed through the Atonement, and the Atonement covers much more than sin. What else does it do? Why do we need to bring them? What does the Atonement do for people?

Sister Reeves: Well, the sorrows that we feel . . .

Sister Stephens: Disappointments and loss . . .

Sister Burton: Strengthens, reconciles, it enables us, doesn't it? We've got to bring them to Him, and they're everywhere. Let's close with our testimonies, should we? Do you want to go first with your testimony, Sister Reeves?

Sister Reeves: I would love to; thank you. Dear sisters, what a sweet experience this has been. I hope you can tell how much we love each other. It was instant. I did not know these two darling, wonderful sisters, and when we first met for the first time, the three of us together, in the bathroom, we were having to dress for photos, of all things . . .

Sister Stephens: We were hiding from everyone!

Sister Reeves: . . . the feeling came over me that we had worked together before. I have to say that every time I walk into that Relief Society building I still expect an alarm to go off and a couple of men to come and take me by the arm and carry me out and say, "What are you doing in here?" And I will say, "I don't know."

But I am so grateful to my Father in Heaven for this opportunity to serve. As you came in today, as I looked out—I said to myself, *Okay, I'm not going to be nervous. I'm going to imagine them all as beautiful colored dots and not think about the fact that they are truly people.* But as I looked into your faces, I realized how much love the Lord has put into my heart for the sisters all over the world, not just sisters of the Church but sisters all over the world—including those that aren't yet members of the Church. I want you to know that I love my Savior. I know that He lives. I know that He stands at the head of The Church of Jesus Christ of Latter-day Saints. I am so grateful to be able to daily repent of my sins, and to become clean again through His atoning sacrifice. I love the Prophet Joseph Smith. I love the Book of Mormon. I am so grateful to live at a time on the earth when we have living prophets, including our dear prophet, President Thomas S. Monson, whom I love.

Sister Stephens: Like Linda, when I walked in—and I do this often when I'm asked to give a talk—I looked into the audience, and looked into the eyes of the sisters, and I asked Heavenly Father to help me to feel His love for you. As I am filled with that love, I also pray that He will help you to feel of His love through me. I'm sure you can't imagine it, but I feel a great deal of peace sitting here in front of you because I feel such a great love, the great love that our Heavenly Father has for you and that I have for you. One of the blessings of this calling is being able to receive and know an extra portion of the love Heavenly Father has for His daughters.

I know that I am a daughter of Heavenly Father, who loves me. That makes all the difference. I know that He has a work for me to do. He has a work for each one of us to do. He loves us so much, He wants us to come back and be with Him again some day, and He's prepared a way for us to be able to do that through His perfect plan. I am so thankful for a Savior who makes it all possible. I am weak and simple—I confess that to each one of you—but I also have faith that's increasing every day, and I love my Savior, and know that in and through and because of Him, I can do what I've been asked to do. I'm so thankful for a prophet—for prophets, seers, and revelators who are the watchmen on the tower, who see the way ahead and can protect us and guide us if we will just listen to them. I'm so grateful for them, thankful for the Restoration of the gospel, for the Prophet Joseph Smith. I know the Book of Mormon is the word of God. It is another testament of Jesus Christ. I'm so thankful to know these things and to be able to bear testimony of them.

Sister Burton: We mentioned at the beginning that our hope for you is that you go home with something specific that you have felt in your hearts. We hope that the Spirit you have felt has filled your spiritual vessel so that you can go home and strengthen your own families, and strengthen those that you live next door to, those that you visit teach, anyone who comes within your sphere of influence. As we speak of our Relief Society purposes, to increase our faith, to strengthen families, and seek out to help others, we speak with one voice. Our united voice helps us to be vital women in the gospel. Our influence for good will be incalculable as we do these things.

We talked about bringing others to Jesus Christ so that His Atonement can heal them. I want to share one statement from Elder Jeffrey R. Holland's April 2012 general conference talk that gives me hope because of the Atonement. He said, "However late you think you are, however many chances you think you have missed, however many mistakes you feel you have made or talents you think you don't have, or however far from home and family and God you feel you have traveled, I testify that you have not traveled beyond the reach of divine love. It is not possible for you to sink lower than the infinite light of Christ's Atonement shines."[12]

I hope each of us believes that in our hearts because it is true. I testify our Father in Heaven lives and loves us. He knows us individually and perfectly—and by name. The greatest evidence of His love is that He sent His Son, Jesus Christ. Christ's Atonement covers everything that is unfair in this life. I testify of Him. I love Him. I thank Him for what He has done for me. I thank you for who you are. And I pray fervently that the Lord will bless each of you. Thank you for your love, for your prayers. We need them desperately, as you can only imagine. May Heavenly Father bless you and strengthen your homes and your families and all those you love.

Notes

1. *The Woman's Exponent,* vol. 6, no. 10 (15 October 1877): 74; available at http://contentdm.lib.byu.edu/cdm/ref/collection/WomansExp/id/6173; accessed 17 October 2012.
2. Joseph Smith, in *Daughters in My Kingdom* (Salt Lake City: The Church of Jesus Christ of Latter-day Saints, 2011), 24.
3. *Daughters in My Kingdom,* xiii.
4. Gary E. Stevenson, "Sacred Homes, Sacred Temples," *Ensign,* May 2009, 101–3.
5. Elaine S. Dalton, "A Return to Virtue," *Ensign,* November 2008, 79.
6. See Ruth Todd, "'Armed with Righteousness and with the Power of God in Great Glory,'" in *Armed with Righteousness: Talks from the 2012 BYU Women's Conference* (Salt Lake City: Deseret Book, 2013), 1–14.
7. Boyd K. Packer, "Counsel to Youth," *Ensign,* November 2011, 18.

8. Smith, in *Daughters in My Kingdom*, 16.
9. M. Russell Ballard, quoting Spencer W. Kimball, "Finding Joy through Loving Service," *Ensign*, May 2011, 48.
10. Ballard, "Women of Righteousness," *Ensign*, April 2002, 70.
11. Letter in author's possession.
12. Jeffrey R. Holland, "The Laborers in the Vineyard," *Ensign*, May 2012, 33.

Our Prayer for Our Granddaughters

Elder Neil L. Andersen and Sister Kathy Andersen

President Thomas S. Monson once began a talk to a conference of women in this way: "I realize that as a man I am in the minority [in this audience]. . . . I feel much the same as the shy country cousin who came to visit his relative in a large cosmopolitan city. He had not [visited his relatives] for some years and was startled when a young boy answered the ringing of the doorbell. The lad asked him in; and after they were comfortably seated, he inquired, 'Who are you, anyway?'

"The visitor answered, 'I'm a cousin on your father's side,' whereupon the boy replied, 'Mister, in this house, that puts you on the wrong side!'"

President Monson continued, "I trust . . . in this house, I might be found on the right side, even the Lord's side."[1]

This is a special kind of conference. Those who attend this conference or watch the delayed broadcast or read the transcribed talks are

---

Elder Neil L. Andersen was called to the Quorum of the Twelve Apostles in April 2009. He was called to the First Quorum of the Seventy in April 1993. He has served in the Presidency of the Seventy, and in area presidencies in Brazil and Europe. He also served as president of the France Bordeaux Mission and as president of the Tampa Florida Stake. He graduated from Brigham Young University, where he was a Hinckley Scholar, and received an MBA from Harvard University.

Sister Kathy Andersen served a mission to the France Bordeaux Mission, and as an early-morning seminary teacher. She has also served on assignment with her husband in his calling. She graduated from Brigham Young University. She and her husband are the parents of four children and have fifteen grandchildren.

devoted disciples of Christ, filled with deep purpose and faith. You are here seeking added strength for today and for the days ahead. I know you have received much from what you have learned. I am humbled and honored to make this presentation. I have come today by assignment of the First Presidency. I pray that the Spirit of the Lord will be with us, and that you might receive the further answers and confirmations you are seeking.

President Boyd K. Packer likes to say: "Young men speak of the future because they have no past, and old men speak of the past because they have no future."[2]

Today I speak as an old man, but I speak of the future. As members of the Quorum of the Twelve, we are to be watchmen on the tower, sounding a warning trumpet that all may hear (see Ezekiel 33:6–7). Because of where we stand, we are to see afar off, and give voice to the dangers ahead.

If you will listen closely today, you will hear a joyful sound from my trumpet. To the righteous, it will be a sound of gladness, of optimism, and of wonderful anticipation for the future.

The theme of our conference comes from the writings of Nephi as he observed the latter days of the earth prior to the Second Coming of the Savior. Like many before and after him, Nephi describes this as a time of wickedness and abominations (see 1 Nephi 14:12), a time when hearts are hardened and minds are blinded toward spiritual truths (see 1 Nephi 14:7). It parallels President Monson's comments that our days are moving away "from that which is spiritual . . . [with] the winds of change [swirling] around us and the moral fiber of society [continuing] to disintegrate before our very eyes."[3]

Wickedness will not diminish as we move toward the final scenes before the Savior's glorious return. Nephi prophesies that the adversary will have "dominion over all the earth, among all nations, kindreds, tongues, and people" (1 Nephi 14:11).

But in the very same verses that speak of these difficulties, Nephi also prophesies of great blessings and the ultimate victory that will come for the righteous. The angel told Nephi that all of this would occur during a time when "the Lamb of God . . . [is working] . . . a marvelous . . . and everlasting [work]" (1 Nephi 14:7) and when He is manifesting Himself in word and in power, bringing peace and eternal life (see 1 Nephi 14:1, 7).

The angel showed Nephi "the church of the Lamb of God." Their numbers were few, but they were "upon all the face of the earth" (1 Nephi 14:12). New stakes have been recently approved not only in the centers of strength of North and South America but also in Asia, the South Pacific, the Caribbean, Africa, and deep in the Amazon forest of Brazil. The day will come when we will honestly be able to declare that the restored gospel of Jesus Christ is upon all the face of the earth.

Nephi described those belonging to the Church as "the saints of God" and the "covenant people of the Lord" (1 Nephi 14:14). The scriptures say that they too had dominions (or places they influence), but they were described as being "small," perhaps meaning principally in their homes, their families, and places closely surrounding them.

In describing these events, Brigham Young said: "It was revealed to me in the commencement of this Church, that the Church would spread, prosper, grow and extend, and that in proportion to the spread of the Gospel among the nations of the earth, so would the power of Satan rise."[4]

To live our mortality at this time is a great privilege. These are great days of destiny and you are an important part in the unfolding events that are occurring and will occur in preparation for the Savior's return.

The angel showed Nephi "multitudes of the earth" in the large and spacious building of Lehi's dream, who had "gathered together to fight against the twelve apostles of the Lamb" (1 Nephi 11:34, 35).

One evening soon after my call to the Quorum of the Twelve, my wife, Kathy, commented, "Neil, I read a verse today in 1 Nephi 11 that speaks of many who are gathered together to fight against the Twelve Apostles of the Lamb." She continued, "I've read that verse many times in the past, but today it seemed so personal and it frightened me."

We sometimes imagine this as physical conflict. The scriptures affirm that there will be "wars, and rumors of wars" (1 Nephi 12:2) upon the earth. They will worsen in the years ahead.

But the physical conflicts will not be our greatest challenge. The spiritual war that is raging for the souls of men and women is much more daunting, with consequences of greater significance.

We recognize the enemy and understand his plan. Nephi said that those of the "great and spacious building," represent the world, and specifically the pride and wisdom of the world (see 1 Nephi 8:26–28).

The pride of the world seeks to destroy faith by casting doubt on the existence of God or, if not His existence, His personal care and concern for His children. It has been a tactic of the adversary since ancient times. Remember the words of Korihor, "I do not deny the existence of a God, but I do not believe that there is a God; and I say also, that ye do not know that there is a God; and except ye show me a sign, I will not believe" (Alma 30:48). Does that sound familiar? To the world, the promise of a Savior and the doctrine of Christ is a foolish tradition (see Alma 30:27).

Nephi describes the large and spacious building as being "vain imaginations" (1 Nephi 12:18). One imagines that his or her own wisdom, his or her own abilities are sufficient, never acknowledging that all he is, all that she has, is dependent upon the goodness of the Father, who is God. *Vain* because one believes the world centers around "me." *Imaginations* because it is so distant from reality. Korihor once again: "Every man [fares] in this life according to the management of the creature; . . . every [woman prospers] according to [her] genius, and . . . every man [conquers] according to his strength" (Alma 30:17).

The prophet Jacob added these insights: "When they are learned they think they are wise, and they hearken not unto the counsel of God, for they set it aside, supposing they know of themselves" (2 Nephi 9:28).

Describing the United States, Ross Douthat said in a *New York Times* editorial in April 2012: "We're neither traditionally Christian nor straightforwardly secular. Instead, we're a nation of heretics in which most people still associate themselves with Christianity but revise its doctrines as they see fit, and nobody can agree on even the most basic definitions of what Christian faith should mean."[5] Many have called this the doctrine of cafeteria Christianity, choosing or discarding doctrine because of personal preference.

Riches can also have a part in the pride of the world. Nephi said that the manner of the dress of those in the spacious building "was exceedingly fine" (1 Nephi 8:27). Jacob describes those whose "hearts are upon their treasures; . . . [whose] treasure is their god" (2 Nephi 9:30).

The spiritual battle rages because those who have chosen wickedness, darkness, and self-conceit are never happy to go their way alone. They form unholy alliances with what Paul calls the principalities, powers, rulers of darkness, and spiritual wickedness in high places (see Ephesians 6:12), determined to take others with them. Nephi explains that they are characterized by scoffing voices, and mocking and pointing fingers (see 1 Nephi 8:27). Jacob adds that "they despise the poor, and they persecute the meek" (2 Nephi 9:30).

And thus, while wanting us all, they especially pursue the young, the unsure, the undisciplined, and the weak, hoping to destroy any "hope of Christ" (1 Corinthians 15:19) in the fragile and vulnerable. You are on the battlefield, right in the crossfire. The conflict will not diminish, but intensify in the years ahead. How will we—how will you—withstand the attack?

The prospects could seem bleak without the power and promises of our Heavenly Father, and His Son, Jesus Christ. The promise of God to us is the theme of this conference.

"And it came to pass that I, Nephi, beheld the power of the Lamb of God, that it descended upon the saints of the church of the Lamb, and upon the covenant people of the Lord, who were scattered upon all the face of the earth; and they were armed with righteousness and with the power of God in great glory" (1 Nephi 14:14).

As you arm yourself for battle, your protection comes from God, who is our Father.

You have faith in the Lord Jesus Christ and take His name upon you. You are commissioned as a disciple of Christ, a defender of the faith. You have heard the words of Paul throughout this conference: "Wherefore take unto you the whole armour of God, that ye may be able to withstand . . .

"Stand therefore, having your loins girt about with truth, and having on the breastplate of righteousness;

"And your feet shod with the preparation of the gospel of peace;

"Above all, taking the shield of faith, wherewith ye shall be able to quench [it doesn't just say *deflect*, it says *quench*] all the fiery darts of the wicked.

"And take the helmet of salvation, and the sword of the Spirit, which is the word of God" (Ephesians 6:13–17).

You are to be armed with "righteousness and the power of God in great glory" (1 Nephi 14:14).

When you are armed with "righteousness and the power of God in great glory," it is because something is happening inside of you, as well as the outward, public display of your discipleship. Your belief in Christ and your love for Him fills your soul. We sometimes refer to this as conversion.

Speaking nearly fifty years ago, Elder Marion G. Romney, who later served in the First Presidency, explained: "Membership in the Church and conversion are not necessarily synonymous. Being converted . . . and having a testimony are not necessarily the same thing either. A testimony comes when the Holy Ghost gives the earnest seeker a witness of the truth. A moving testimony vitalizes faith; that is, it induces repentance and obedience to the commandments. Conversion . . . is the fruit of, or the reward for, repentance and obedience."[6] Conversion is a process, and usually requires an extended time of righteousness.

Jesus said to Peter, "When thou art converted, strengthen thy brethren" (Luke 22:32).

We sometimes use descriptive phrases with the word *converted*; for example, "fully converted" or "completely converted." The best description I know is found in the Book of Mormon where we learn that when the Lamanites "were converted unto the Lord, [they] never did fall away" (Alma 23:6). Conversion requires daily nourishment and renewal.

In one of Elder Neal A. Maxwell's last essays, written shortly before his passing, he said, "We use the words *baptism, testimony*, and *conversion* carelessly, even interchangeably. Yet baptism is an *event*, whereas conversion is a *process*.

"There can be baptism without testimony. There can be testimony without engaging in the process of becoming even as Jesus is (see 3 Nephi 27:27), but there cannot be conversion without testimony and without baptism by fire and water (see D&C 33:11)."[7]

Think about the journey of your own conversion and discipleship through the years. When you are more sensitive in taking His name upon you, seeking the spiritual gifts from His sacred ordinances, and giving added care to following Him, you feel greater strength. You see more clearly, sense more deeply your identity as a daughter of God, and realize in greater measure the purposes you have accomplished, are accomplishing, and will yet accomplish.

Armed with righteousness, the Lord's power through the gift of the Holy Ghost is magnified and elevated in you. Angels and miracles surround you. You are armed with the power of God in great glory. Happiness and peace follow even in times of difficulty. Jesus said, "These things I have spoken unto you, that in me ye might have peace. In the world ye shall have tribulation: but be of good cheer; I have overcome the world" (John 16:33).

We are so grateful for who you are, and for your devotion to the Lord, Jesus Christ, and His work upon the earth. Daily we see your influence for good upon your families, friends, and others who come into your path. Thank you. Thank you for who you are, and who you are becoming. "In the strength of the Lord" you do not give up. "We are *all* enlisted till the conflict is over."[8]

I testify to you that God our Father is a God of miracles. We know something that is almost never known in a raging war. We know that victory is assured. Nephi testifies: "And it came to pass that I saw and bear record, that the great and spacious building was the pride of the world; *and it fell,* and the fall thereof was exceedingly great. And the angel of the Lord spake unto me again, saying: Thus shall be the destruction of all nations, kindreds, tongues, and people, that shall fight against the twelve apostles of the Lamb" (1 Nephi 11:36).

To my Kathy, and to each of you, I assure you that while the battle rages, we need not fear. The Lord will help you, your family, and others you love who need special help. We know the outcome. The Savior will triumph over all!

Hold tight to King Benjamin's declaration: "There shall be no other name given nor any other way nor means whereby salvation can come unto the children of men, only in and through the name of Christ, the Lord Omnipotent" (Mosiah 3:17).

Let me emphasize: You are absolutely critical to this cause! We sometimes like to separate ourselves into groups: men and women, married and single, old and young, rich and poor. The list goes on and on. We wonder about our place—where do we fit?

I pray that the importance of this noble cause will allow less thinking of differences, and more thinking of these great purposes of God now and in the days ahead. You are needed. Whatever your own particular situation, your talents, your faith, your unselfishness, your discipleship are needed.

Uniting together from different backgrounds, countries, cultures, and life experiences, you help advance the stone cut without hands as it rolls forth to fill the whole earth (see D&C 65:2).

"Shall we not go on in so great a cause? Go forward and not backward. Courage, . . . and on, on to the victory!" (D&C 128:22).

I look forward to the future. I hope you do as well. To your children and grandchildren, your friends and associates, you can speak about the future with optimism, joy, and anticipation. You are living your mortality in a glorious time of destiny.

Lest you think my positive feelings are misplaced, let me assure you that I share my optimism with the prophets of God. First, I will tell you an experience I had with President Gordon B. Hinckley.

Just before the general conference of April 2007, all the General Authorities of the Church along with the eight Quorums of the Seventy from around the world were gathered together. It would be President Hinckley's final talk to the general priesthood leadership of the Church—from fifty nations speaking thirty-one different languages.

He delivered a powerfully positive message. Among other things, he said: "We have every reason to be encouraged, and I would like to say that this is only the beginning. Things will get better and better and better as we spread over the earth. I have a strong testimony of that.

"We are still persecuted a little. . . . We don't need to worry about that. If the time ever comes that people don't speak critically about us, I will begin to worry. The Lord's work has always been opposed, and it always will be opposed. It has been opposed since the great war in heaven. That will go on and on and on. But in spite of that, the work will grow ever stronger, affecting for good the lives of people across the world."

He continued, "It is a miracle. . . . The way this Church has expanded over the earth. . . . I believe that all this growth is only the beginning. . . . I am now an old man in my ninety-seventh year. I will not live to see it, but many of you men will." (President Hinckley passed away ten months later.) He continued, "You will see the Church expand in a remarkable and miraculous way, both at home and abroad. What has happened before will be but prologue to what will happen hereafter. . . . As . . . darkness increases the sunlight of the gospel will grow brighter and brighter."

President Hinckley concluded, "Be assured that this is the Lord's work. He will be our ever present friend. He will be our helper in time of need. He will magnify and bless us, comfort us and sustain us. He will not forsake us if we do not forsake Him."[9]

The day following this moving address, I found myself sitting across from President Hinckley at lunch. As a member of the Presidency of the Seventy at the time, it was unusual for me to be so close to the prophet. I searched for the right words to speak. Then I thought of his message from the day before. "President," I said, "that was quite a positive, optimistic talk you gave yesterday."

He put his soup spoon down, looked up at me with somewhat of an incredulous look, and raising the level of his voice just a little, said, "Well, Brother Andersen, I believe it!"

"Me too!" I declared, "100 percent! I believe it too!"

President Thomas S. Monson speaks with great hope and optimism about the future. Were we not all lifted by these inspiring words? "I testify to you that our promised blessings are beyond measure. Though the storm clouds may gather, though the rains may pour down upon us, our knowledge of the gospel and our love of our Heavenly Father and of our Savior will comfort and sustain us and bring joy to our hearts as we walk uprightly and keep the commandments. There will be nothing in this world that can defeat us. . . . Fear not. Be of good cheer. The future is as bright as your faith. . . . Heaven's blessings await us."[10]

Kathy and I titled our message to you "Our Prayer for Our Granddaughters." Why such a title? First, I needed to find a way for you to see pictures of some of our grandchildren. Of our fifteen grandchildren, here are our four granddaughters: Caroline, Saylor, Courtney, and Claire. Aren't they beautiful? Kathy will share our prayers for them, and for our grandsons, in the context of these principles. Kathy, in my totally unbiased viewpoint, is the most wonderful, caring, and beloved grandmother in the world. For more than thirty-seven years I have marveled at her

Photo courtesy Elder Neil L. Andersen.

From left to right: Caroline Hadlock, Saylor Andersen, Courtney Ebert, and Claire Hadlock.

goodness, faith, and spiritual depth. Her devotion to the gospel of Jesus Christ and to me as her eternal companion are remarkable. With sensitivity and power she has taught our children and grandchildren the truths of eternity. Words cannot describe the measure of love I feel for her. Kathy, I love you very much.

Sister Andersen: I love my husband. I am grateful for the privilege of accompanying him today. We are honored to be in your presence.

Last week our three-year-old grandson David expressed some concerns to his mother before going to bed. As he knelt to pray, he spent an unusual amount of time, for a three-year-old, praying to his Heavenly Father about his concern. When he finished his prayer David looked up at his mother and reverently said, "Mommy, He heared me."

Our prayer for our granddaughters is that they will be armed with the power of God in their lives knowing that our Heavenly Father loves us and that He will always hear our prayers.

Many years ago I read a story about a group of Latter-day Saints in a faraway land who had prepared for six months for a visit from the prophet of God. When he arrived in their country those humble, faithful Saints had a remarkable experience that blessed their lives and future generations. Their faith, their love for the prophet, and their effort to prepare themselves for his visit made a deep impression on me.

Just two weeks ago we were in the city of Aguascalientes, Mexico. I met a beautiful grandmother after the conference. She told me that when she learned that a member of the Quorum of the Twelve would speak in their stake, she wanted to do something special to prepare for that day. She decided to read the Book of Mormon from cover to cover. With a big smile, she said, "I finished the Book of Mormon yesterday." For six weeks she had prepared. On that Sunday she had dressed in her very best clothes. With her little granddaughter by her side, she came to hear the word of the Lord through the voice of His servant.

Our prayer for our granddaughters is that they will be armed with righteousness as they believe and have faith in the words of those who are called and ordained to declare His holy word.

On Tuesday of this week, our granddaughter Saylor was baptized. On Wednesday our granddaughter Claire was baptized. They looked so beautiful. Their eyes were bright as they were confirmed by their fathers as members of The Church of Jesus Christ of Latter-day Saints and received the gift of the Holy Ghost.

The gift of the Holy Ghost is a holy gift, a sacred gift, a gift from God that becomes more precious with time and experience. Saylor and Claire are just beginning the experience of having the Comforter as a constant companion. What greater gift could we receive than the presence of a member of the Godhead in our lives to guide us, direct us, comfort us throughout our days of mortality—especially now in these days? This precious, priceless, sacred gift was received by our two eight-year-old granddaughters this week.

On the other end of life's spectrum, we recently visited my husband's mother, Kathryn Andersen. She is eighty-nine years old. As we visited with her she spoke of an impression she had about something she should do for her neighbors.

Whether eight or eighty-nine, our prayer for our granddaughters is that they will live each day of their lives mindful of this sacred gift and that they might "always have his Spirit to be with them" (Moroni 4:3; D&C 20:77).

When I was the age of our granddaughters, my mother, Martha Williams, taught me "that it is upon the rock of our Redeemer, who is Christ, the Son of God, that ye must build your foundation; that when the devil shall send forth his mighty winds, yea, his shafts in the whirlwind, yea, when all his hail and his mighty storm shall beat upon you, it shall have no power over you to drag you down to the gulf of misery and endless wo, because of the rock upon which ye are built, which is a sure foundation, a foundation whereon if men build they cannot fall" (Helaman 5:12).

I realize now that my mother knew something of the mighty winds, the shafts in the whirlwind, the adversary's hail and mighty storm. She began preparing me when I was a child for whatever my future would hold by helping me to build my foundation on Christ, the Son of God.

Several years ago my husband told the story of Hadley Peay. She is a family friend. Hadley is now eleven years old. She "was born with a very serious hearing impairment requiring extensive surgery to bring even limited hearing. Her parents followed with tireless training to help her learn to speak. . . .

"Once, when Hadley was four, she was standing in the checkout line at the grocery store with her mother. She looked behind her and saw a little boy sitting in a wheelchair. She noticed that the boy did not have legs.

"Although Hadley had learned to speak, she had difficulty controlling the volume of her voice. In her louder voice, she asked her mother why the little boy did not have legs.

"Her mother quietly and simply explained to Hadley that 'Heavenly Father makes all of His children different.' 'OK,' Hadley replied.

"Then, unexpectedly, Hadley turned to the little boy in the wheelchair and said, 'Did you know that when Heavenly Father made me, my ears did not work? That makes me special. He made you with no legs, and that makes you special. When Jesus comes, I will be able to hear and you will get your legs. Jesus will make everything all right.'"[11]

We pray that our granddaughters will come to know for themselves with absolute certainty the truthfulness of words spoken by an Apostle of the Lord this day that Jesus is the Christ, the Son of God—that He is our Savior and Redeemer.

Elder Andersen: In the same chapter where we find the theme for our conference, Nephi spoke of the writings that would come later from the Apostle John. Nephi testified of John's mission and of his words concerning the Second Coming of the Savior. Let me conclude with a few verses from the Book of Revelation:

"And I heard as it were the voice of a great multitude, and as the voice of many waters, and as the voice of mighty thunderings, saying, Alleluia: for the Lord God omnipotent reigneth" (Revelation 19:6).

"And he hath on his vesture . . . a name written, KING OF KINGS, AND LORD OF LORDS" (Revelation 19:16).

"And I saw a great white throne, and him that sat on it, from whose face the earth and the heaven fled away" (Revelation 20:11).

"And he said . . . It is done. I am Alpha and Omega, the beginning and the end. . . .

"He that overcometh shall inherit all things; and I will be his God" (Revelation 21:6–7).

"And I saw the dead, small and great, stand before God; and the books were opened: and another book was opened, which is the book of life: and the dead were judged out of those things which were written in the books, according to their works" (Revelation 20:12).

"And I heard a great voice out of heaven saying, Behold, the tabernacle of God is with men, and he will dwell with them, and they shall be his people, and God himself shall be with them, and be their God.

"And God shall wipe away all tears from their eyes; and there shall be no more death, neither sorrow, nor crying, neither shall there be any more pain" (Revelation 21:3–4).

"[And] blessed and holy is he that hath part in the first resurrection" (Revelation 20:6).

"And they shall see his face; and his name shall be in their foreheads.

"And there shall be no night there; and they need no candle, neither light of the sun; for the Lord God giveth them light: and they shall reign for ever and ever" (Revelation 22:4–5).

I testify with the certainty of my apostolic calling that Jesus is the Christ, the light and life of the world. As you devote yourself to Him, as you listen to Him, seek to be more like Him and follow Him, His reality will burn like nothing else inside of you. You will know as certain as you know you live that He lives, and that His promises of life eternal are true and certain. You have great gifts of teaching the gospel to others, and I pray that your testimony of Christ, your conversion to Christ, will sink deeply into the hearts of those you are close to. I pray that you may receive His personal approval, knowing that the Lord has blessed you to set someone else upon an eternal course.

He will come again. We shall see His face, and His name shall be upon us. May we look forward with faith. May we be worthy to bear His name.

NOTES

1. Thomas S. Monson, "If Ye Are Prepared Ye Shall Not Fear," *Ensign*, November 2004, 113.
2. Boyd K. Packer, "Counsel to Young Men," *Ensign*, May 2009, 49.
3. Thomas S. Monson, "Stand in Holy Places," *Ensign*, November 2011, 83, 86.
4. Brigham Young, in *Journal of Discourses*, 26 vols. (Liverpool: Latter-day Saints' Book Depot, 1854–86), 13:280.
5. Ross Douthat, "Divided by God," *New York Times*, 7 April 2012; available at http://www.nytimes.com/2012/04/08/opinion/sunday/douthat-in-2012-no-religious-center-is-holding.html?pagewanted=all&_r=0; accessed 29 October 2012.
6. Marion G. Romney, in Conference Report, October 1963, 24.
7. Neal A. Maxwell, *Moving in His Majesty and Power* (Salt Lake City: Deseret Book, 2004), 41.
8. Anonymous, "We Are All Enlisted," *Hymns of The Church of Jesus Christ of Latter-day Saints* (Salt Lake City: The Church of Jesus Christ of Latter-day Saints, 1985), no. 250; emphasis added.
9. Gordon B. Hinckley, comments during General Authority and Area Seventy Training, 29 March 2007.
10. Thomas S. Monson, "Be of Good Cheer," *Ensign*, May 2009, 92.
11. Neil L. Andersen, "You Know Enough," *Ensign*, November 2008, 14.

INDEX